Personal Tax

(Finance Act 2024)

Workbook

For assessments from 27 January 2025

Aubrey Penning
Bob Thomas

© Aubrey Penning, Bob Thomas, 2024.

All rights reserved. No part of this publication may be reproduced, stored in a retrieval system, or transmitted in any form or by any means, electronic, mechanical, photo-copying, recording or otherwise, without the prior consent of the copyright owners, or in accordance with the provisions of the Copyright, Designs and Patents Act 1988, or under the terms of any licence permitting limited copying issued by the Copyright Licensing Agency, Saffron House, 6-10 Kirby Street, London EC1N 8TS.

Published by Osborne Books Limited
Tel 01905 748071
Email books@osbornebooks.co.uk
Website www.osbornebooks.co.uk

Design by Laura Ingham

Printed by CPI Group (UK) Limited, Croydon, CR0 4YY, on environmentally friendly, acid-free paper from managed forests.

British Library Cataloguing in Publication Data
A catalogue record for this book is available from the British Library

ISBN 978-1-911681-13-7

Contents

Introduction

Chapter activities

1	Introduction to Income Tax	2
2	Income from property	6
3	Income from savings and investments	9
4	Income from employment	11
5	Preparing Income Tax computations	15
6	Capital Gains Tax	19
7	Inheritance Tax	23

Answers to chapter activities   25

Practice assessments

Practice assessment 1	39
Practice assessment 2	53
Practice assessment 3	67

Answers to practice assessments

Practice assessment 1	81
Practice assessment 2	89
Practice assessment 3	95

AAT Reference Material

Taxation tables	101
Professional conduct in relation to taxation	109

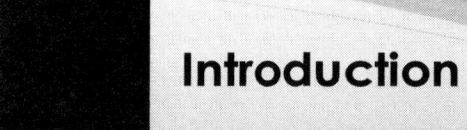

Introduction

Qualifications covered

This book has been written specifically to cover the Unit 'Personal Tax' which is optional for the following qualifications:

AAT Level 4 Diploma in Professional Accounting

AAT Diploma in Professional Accounting – SCQF Level 8

This book contains Chapter Activities which provide extra practice material in addition to the activities included in the Osborne Books Tutorial text, and Practice Assessments to prepare the student for the computer based assessments. The latter are based directly on the structure, style and content of the sample assessment material provided by the AAT at www.aat.org.uk.

Suggested answers to the Chapter Activities and Practice Assessments are set out in this book.

Osborne Study and Revision Materials

Additional materials, tailored to the needs of students studying this unit and revising for the assessment, include:

- **Tutorials:** paperback books with practice activities
- **Student Zone:** access to Osborne Books online resources
- **Osborne Books App:** Osborne Books ebooks for mobiles and tablets

Visit www.osbornebooks.co.uk for details of study and revision resources and access to online material.

Exams, Finance Acts and tax years

This book has been designed to include guidance and exercises based on Tax Year 2024/25 (Finance Act 2024). We understand that the AAT plans to assess this legislation from January 2025 to January 2026. Tutors and students are advised to check dates with the AAT and ensure that they sit the correct computer based assessment.

Chapter activities

1 Introduction to Income Tax

1.1 State whether each of the following statements is true or false.

		True	False
(a)	Different tax systems are based on different views of which are the most important tax principles and how they should be applied	✓	
(b)	The principle of equity means that every taxpayer should pay the same amount of tax, regardless of their circumstances		✓
(c)	Vertical equity means that taxation is fair at different levels in society	✓	
(d)	Although tax is often used in an attempt to change behaviour, this conflicts with the principle of neutrality	✓	
(e)	A progressive tax system is one in which the same proportion of income is paid in tax for all income levels		✓
(f)	A tax system that charges every taxpayer the same percentage of their income in tax is a proportional system	✓	

1.2 State whether each of the following statements is true or false.

		True	False
(a)	It is not the taxpayer's responsibility to inform HMRC of any untaxed taxable income, unless they have been asked to complete a tax return		✓
(b)	Accountants must normally follow the rules of confidentiality, but there are exceptions	✓	
(c)	Where a practitioner has knowledge or suspicion that his client is money laundering, then he has a duty to inform the relevant person or authority	✓	
(d)	Accountants should warn clients if they suspect money laundering, to give the client a chance to cease the activity		✓
(e)	When an accountant is advising a client, the greatest duty of care is to the client	✓	

1.3 State which of the following can provide sources of information about tax law and its interpretation.

		Yes	No
(a)	HMRC extra-statutory concessions		
(b)	Statute law		
(c)	HMRC statements of practice		
(d)	Case law		
(e)	Website www.gov.uk		
(f)	HMRC guides and help sheets		

1.4 Match the following examples of income with the correct income category.

Sample Income
UK dividends
Partnership profits
Rents from land
Earnings from a job

Income Category
Property Income
Savings and Investment Income
Trading Income
Employment, Pension and Social Security Income

1.5 Tick the columns to show which of the following categories of income is taxed on an accruals basis, and which is normally on a receipts basis (ie based on when received).

Income Category		Accruals basis	Receipts basis
(a)	Property Income		
(b)	Savings and Investment Income		
(c)	Employment, Pension and Social Security Income		

1.6 State which of the following types of income are exempt from Income Tax.

Income Category		Exempt	Not exempt
(a)	Employment Income		✓
(b)	Income from an ISA	✓	
(c)	Premium bond prizes	✓	
(d)	Rent received from a buy-to-let property		✓
(e)	Betting winnings (unless a professional gambler)	✓	
(f)	Lottery prizes	✓	

1.7 Analyse the following list of statements by ticking the appropriate column.

	Statement	True	False
(a)	UK residence is determined by some specific tests that are applied to the individual for each tax year	✓	
(b)	An individual who lives permanently in the UK can choose the domicile of any country in the world, simply by completing the relevant form		✓
(c)	An individual who is resident and domiciled in the UK will pay UK tax on their worldwide income and gains	✓	
(d)	An individual who is resident in the UK, but not UK domiciled or 'deemed domiciled' will pay UK tax on income and gains arising in the UK	✓	
(e)	An individual who is resident in the UK, but not UK domiciled or 'deemed domiciled', will never pay UK tax on income and gains arising in the rest of the world		✓
(f)	An individual who is resident in the UK, but not UK domiciled or 'deemed domiciled', can elect to pay UK tax on their overseas income on a remittance basis, but there is normally a substantial charge for this basis to apply	✓	

1.8 John is self-employed and works both in the UK and Germany. He has a flat in the UK which is always available, and he uses it when he is in the country. He also has a house in Germany where his wife and child live (they are not UK residents). He was a UK resident in 2022/23 (when he spent 140 days in the UK), but not in 2023/24.

In 2024/25 John spent 115 days in the UK working. He spent the rest of the year in Germany.

Using the appropriate tests, decide whether John is a UK resident for 2024/25.

2 Income from property

2.1 Chester has two properties in addition to his home, details of which are as follows:

Two bedroom house:

(1) This unfurnished house is rented out for £850 per month payable on the 6th of each month. The property was occupied this tax year until 1 February when the tenants suddenly moved out, owing the rent for January. Chester knows that he will not recover this rent. The property was let again from 1 May to another family.

(2) Chester had to pay £530 for redecoration in March following the poor condition of the property at that time.

(3) The only other expense paid by Chester on the house was a 10% management charge to the agent on rent received.

One bedroom flat:

(1) This furnished flat is rented out for £550 per month. The property was rented all tax year.

(2) Chester paid council tax and water rates on the flat, totalling £1,100 for the period that the flat was occupied. He also paid buildings and contents insurance of £340 for the year.

Calculate the profit or loss made on each property, using the following table.

	Two bedroom house £	One bedroom flat £
Income		
Expenses:		

2.2 Stephan rents out one furnished property. The following is a statement compiled from his accounting records relating to the tax year.

	£	£
Rental Income Received		12,000
less expenditure:		
Council Tax	700	
Water Rates	300	
Insurance	380	
Cost of replacement furniture	2,100	
Depreciation of furniture	800	
Managing Agent's Charges	1,200	
		5,480
Profit		6,520

Required:

Calculate the assessable property income for Stephan, using the following table.

	£	£
Income		
Expenditure:		
Assessable Income		

2.3 The following list of expenditure relates to a rental property.

Analyse the expenditure according to its tax treatment.

Expenditure		Allowable	Not allowable
(a)	Replacement of washing machine		
(b)	Legal fees relating to purchase of property		
(c)	Cleaning property between tenancies		
(d)	Legal fees relating to tenancy agreement		
(e)	Renovation of property between purchase and first tenancy		
(f)	Insurance against non-recoverable rent		

2.4 The following expenditure was incurred during a void period between tenancies.

Analyse the expenditure according to its tax treatment.

Expenditure		Allowable	Not allowable
(a)	Internal redecoration		
(b)	Replacement of carpets		
(c)	Council tax		
(d)	Property insurance		
(e)	Building an extension		
(f)	Advertising for tenants		

3 Income from savings and investments

3.1 Analyse the following statements into those that are true and those that are false.

		True	False
(a)	There is no dividend allowance available for additional rate taxpayers		
(b)	Income that falls within the personal savings allowance will still be treated as using up the tax bands and can result in savings or dividend income being pushed into a higher tax band		
(c)	There is no personal savings allowance available for additional rate taxpayers		
(d)	The personal savings allowance can be used to save tax on savings income or dividend income		

3.2 An individual has the following income before deduction of the personal allowance:

General Income   £20,070

Savings Income   £1,500

Dividend Income   £2,000

Calculate the amount of Income Tax payable on each of these categories of income, and in total.

3.3 An individual has the following income before deduction of the personal allowance:

General Income   £25,070

Savings Income   £3,500

Dividend Income   £6,000

Calculate the amount of Income Tax payable on each of these categories of income, and in total.

3.4 An individual has the following income before deduction of the personal allowance:

General Income £60,000

Savings Income £7,500

Dividend Income £5,000

Calculate the amount of Income Tax payable on each of these categories of income, and in total.

3.5 The following statements relate to Individual Savings Accounts (ISAs). Identify which statements are true and which are false.

			True	False
	(a)	Cash ISAs can only be opened by individuals who are UK resident		
	(b)	Stocks and shares ISAs can be used for shares in listed companies and government securities (gilts)		
	(c)	The interest and/or dividends received from investment in ISAs are tax-free and do not utilise the personal savings allowance or dividend allowance		
	(d)	Cash ISAs can only be transferred to another provider at the end of a tax year		
	(e)	ISAs cannot be held in joint names, and individual investors must be UK resident		

4 Income from employment

4.1 Complete the following table by correctly matching the indicators as relating to employment or self-employment.

Indicators of Employment	Indicators of Self-Employment

Indicators

- Choose work hours and invoice for work done   SE
- Need to do the work yourself   E
- Told how, where and when to do work   E
- No risk of capital or losses   E
- Work for several people or organisations   SE
- Decide yourself how, when and where to do work   SE
- Can employ helper or substitute   SE
- Employer provides equipment   E
- Risk own capital and bear losses from work that is not to standard   SE
- Work set hours and paid regular wage with sick pay and holidays   E
- Usually work for one employer   E
- Provide own equipment   SE

4.2 (a) What scale charge percentage would be applied for petrol or hybrid cars with the following CO_2 emissions?

(1) 44 g/km (electric range 25 miles)

(2) 134 g/km

(3) 151 g/km

(4) 249 g/km

(b) Silvia was provided with a secondhand car on 6 October 2024. It cost the company £8,000, but the list price of this car when bought new was £17,000. The car has a CO_2 emission of 148 g/km, and has a diesel engine which is not RDE2 compliant. The company pays for all running costs, except private fuel.

(1) The cost of the car used in the benefit in kind computation is

£ [ ]

(2) The percentage used in the benefit in kind computation is

[ ] %

(3) The assessable benefit for Silvia relating to the car for 2024/25 is

£ [ ]

4.3 (a) When accommodation is purchased by an employer, what is the value of the property above which an additional benefit is applied?

(a)	£60,000	
(b)	£70,000	
(c)	£75,000	
(d)	£80,000	
(e)	£100,000	
(f)	£125,000	

(b) Would the following situations be treated as being job-related where no accommodation benefit arises?

Indicators of Employment		Yes	No
(a)	House provided for a vicar		
(b)	House provided by employer for accountant working for a housing association		
(c)	Flat in sheltered accommodation provided for an on-site care manager		

(c) Summer was provided with accommodation in the form of a flat that the employer purchased recently for £165,000. It is not job-related. The flat has an annual value of £9,300. Summer pays £200 per month towards the private use of the flat. Assume that the HMRC official interest rate is 2.25%. Her taxable benefit is:

(a)	£6,900	
(b)	£9,300	
(c)	£8,925	
(d)	£11,325	

4.4 On 6 December 2024, Kevin was provided with a company loan of £16,000 on which he pays interest at 1.0% per annum. On 6 February 2025 Kevin repaid £2,000. The official rate of interest is 2.25%.

What is the benefit in kind for 2024/25 rounded down to the £?

4.5 (a) Dee uses her own car for business travelling. During the tax year she travelled 11,500 business miles for which she was paid 50p per mile by her employer. The impact of this is:

(a)	She will have a taxable amount of £575	
(b)	She will have a taxable amount of £875	
(c)	She will claim an allowable expense of £875	
(d)	She will claim an allowable expense of £575	

(b) Eddle has an occupational pension scheme to which he contributes 5% of his salary. His employer contributes 6% of his salary. His salary was £28,400. The impact of this is:

(a)	His taxable salary will be increased by £1,704	
(b)	His taxable salary will be reduced by £1,420	✓
(c)	His taxable salary will be increased by £284	
(d)	His basic rate band will be extended by £1,775	

(c) Steve pays £300 per year in subscriptions to professional bodies. His employer reimburses him £180. The overall impact of this is:

(a)	No impact on tax	
(b)	An allowable deduction of £120	
(c)	A benefit of £180	
(d)	An allowable deduction of £300	

(d) Genna has a non-contributory occupational pension scheme. This means:

(a)	The employer pays a percentage of her salary into the scheme, but Genna does not	
(b)	Genna pays a percentage of her salary into the scheme, but the employer does not	
(c)	Only the Government pays a percentage of her salary into the scheme	
(d)	Genna and the Government both pay a percentage of her salary into the scheme	

5 Preparing Income Tax computations

5.1 John has the following income for the tax year:

Employment Income	£57,500
Rental Income	£10,350
Bank account interest	£700
Dividends	£6,500

John paid £3,200 (net) into a private pension scheme, and made gift aid payments totalling £1,600 (net).

Using the following table, calculate the total Income Tax liability for John.

	£
Employment Income	
Rental Income	
Savings Income	
Dividend Income	
less Personal Allowance	
Taxable Income	
Tax Calculation:	

5.2 Dave and Sue are a married couple with a joint savings account that produces annual savings income of £4,000. They have no other savings income.

Dave has general income of £20,000, and Sue has general income of £55,000.

Complete the following table to show for each person the annual Income Tax on the savings income only, based on three alternative situations:

- The current situation
- If all the savings were held in Dave's name
- If all the savings were held in Sue's name

Situation	Dave's tax on savings income £	Sue's tax on savings income £
Current position		
All savings in Dave's name		
All savings in Sue's name		

5.3 Karen has employment income of £50,000, plus normal profits from a rental property of £8,000 per year. She is considering whether to spend an additional £6,000 on replacement carpets and curtains for the rental property. She does not claim the property allowance.

Complete the following table.

	Normal situation £	Replacing carpet and curtains £
Taxable Income		
Tax at 20%		
Tax at 40%		
Total Income Tax		
Net Cost of Replacements		

5.4 Wayne earns £45,000 per year from his job as a Sales Manager, and is entitled to a diesel company car (RDE2 compliant) and all fuel (business and private). The car has a list price of £22,000, but was purchased at a discount for £19,500. It has emissions of 144 g/km.

Wayne makes cash contributions of £1,600 per year into a personal pension scheme.

Calculate Wayne's tax liability (to the nearest £), using the following table.

Include any workings:	
	£
Salary	
Car benefit	
Fuel benefit	
Personal allowance	
Taxable Income	
Tax at 20%:	
Tax at 40%:	
Total tax liability	

5.5 Rachel had employment income of £91,500 and received dividends of £17,500. She paid £1,200 (net) into a personal pension scheme.

Calculate her total Income Tax liability (ie before deduction of tax paid) for the tax year, using the table given below. Show tax to the nearest £.

	£
Employment Income	
Dividends	
Personal allowance	
Taxable Income	

6 Capital Gains Tax

6.1 For each statement, tick the appropriate box.

		Actual proceeds used	Deemed proceeds used	No gain or loss basis
(a)	Father gives an asset to his son		✓	
(b)	Wife sells an asset to her husband			✓
(c)	Simon gives an asset to his friend		✓	
(d)	Margaret sells an asset to her cousin for £15,000 when the market value is £40,000	✓		
(e)	Brian gives an asset to his civil partner, Dave			✓

6.2 Alex bought an asset in January 2008 for £36,000, selling it in the tax year for £35,000. He paid auctioneer's commission of 4% when he bought the asset and 5% when he sold the asset.

The loss on this asset is:

(a)	£nil	
(b)	£1,000	
(c)	£4,190	
(d)	£2,440	

Legal fees are an allowable deduction where they relate to the purchase or sale of an asset.

TRUE / FALSE

6.3 State whether each of the following statements is true or false:

		True	False
(a)	The annual exemption is applied after capital losses are deducted		
(b)	Capital losses from the same year cannot safeguard the annual exemption		
(c)	Capital losses can be set against gains of the previous tax year		
(d)	Capital losses brought forward can safeguard the annual exemption when offset against current year gains		

6.4 Josie has a capital loss brought forward of £10,000. She is a higher rate Income Tax payer.

She sold an asset during the tax year for £19,000. She had been given the asset by her husband when it was worth £8,000. Her husband originally paid £6,500 for the asset.

Complete the following sentences:

(a) The gain on the asset is £ ☐

(b) The amount of loss that will be relieved is £ ☐

(c) The Capital Gains Tax payable is £ ☐

(d) The loss to be carried forward to the next tax year is £ ☐

6.5 Complete the following table to show which assets are exempt from Capital Gains Tax and which are chargeable.

Asset	Exempt	Chargeable
Antique furniture valued at £30,000		
Main private residence		
Clock		
Shares		
Holiday home		
Government securities		
Vintage car		
Land		

6.6 Richard bought a house on 1 January 2006 for £125,000. He lived in the house until 31 December 2008 when he moved abroad for one year to work. He returned from abroad on 31 December 2009, and then immediately moved into his elderly father's house until 30 June 2011, leaving his own home empty. He then moved back into his own house until 31 December 2018, when he moved to a new home and put the house on the market. The house was eventually sold on 1 January 2025 for £205,000.

(a) Which periods are treated as occupied and which are not?

Occupation / Deemed Occupation	Non-occupation
1 Jan 2006 – 31 Dec 2008: actual occupation (3 years / 36 months)	1 Jan 2019 – 31 March 2024: non-occupation (63 months)
1 Jan 2009 – 31 Dec 2009: deemed occupation – working abroad (12 months)	
1 Jan 2010 – 30 June 2011: deemed occupation – up to 3 years any reason (18 months)	
1 July 2011 – 31 Dec 2018: actual occupation (90 months)	
1 April 2024 – 1 Jan 2025: deemed occupation – last 9 months of ownership	
Total: 165 months	Total: 63 months

(b) What is the chargeable gain on the property?

£ 22,105

6.7 The following table relates to sales of chattels.

Match the statements shown below to the correct asset details.

Asset	Sale proceeds	Cost	Statement
1	£4,000	£7,000	
2	£14,000	£8,000	
3	£8,000	£3,000	
4	£3,000	£5,000	
5	£15,000	£21,000	

Statements:

- Exempt asset
- Calculate gain as normal
- Calculate loss as normal
- Sale proceeds to be £6,000
- Chattel marginal relief applies

6.8 Paul bought 20,000 shares in Lincoln Ltd for £5 per share in October 2000. He received a bonus issue of 1 for 25 shares in March 2003. In January 2025, Paul sold 8,000 shares for £9 per share.

Clearly showing the balance of shares, and their value, to carry forward, calculate the gain made on these shares. All workings must be shown in your calculations.

7 Inheritance Tax

7.1 Elizabeth died, leaving an estate of £800,000. She had not made any lifetime transfers. In her will she left the following:

- £250,000 to her husband, Phil
- £2,000 to charity
- The balance of her estate to her son, Robert, including a home worth £300,000.

Calculate the Inheritance Tax due on the estate, and how much Robert will receive.

7.2 Paul and Mary had been married for several years, when Mary died. Mary had not made any lifetime transfers. Mary left £40,000 to each of their two sons and the balance to Paul, including a home. Mary's estate was valued at £350,000.

Three years after Mary's death, Paul died. He had not made any lifetime transfers. His estate was worth £950,000 including a home worth £350,000, to be divided equally between his two sons.

Calculate the Inheritance Tax due on:

- Mary's estate
- Paul's estate

7.3 Christine did not make any lifetime transfers in the previous tax year. During the current tax year she made the following gifts (shown in chronological order):

- £10,000 to her daughter, Rosy, when she got married
- £5,000 to her son, Robert, when he got divorced
- £1,000 to charity
- £500 to the Labour Party
- £2,500 to her parents to pay for them to go on holiday
- £15,000 to her husband, Roger, to buy a new car

Calculate the amount of each potentially exempt transfer made in the current tax year. Show clearly the use of each annual exemption where applicable.

7.4 Jonathan (who had not made any other transfers in recent tax years) made the following lifetime transfers:

31 December 2022	£170,000 payment into a trust (a chargeable transfer)
30 April 2023	£20,000 to his son, David
31 May 2023	£30,000 to his daughter Masie on her birthday

On 30 September 2024, Jonathan died and left an estate valued at £630,000. It did not include a home. Jonathan's will listed the following beneficiaries:

- £250,000 to be paid to his wife, Julie
- £5,000 to be given to charity
- The balance to be shared equally between David and Masie

Calculate:

- The Inheritance Tax payable during Jonathan's lifetime
- The Inheritance Tax payable on Jonathan's death

7.5 Jim had made no lifetime transfers. When he died he left an estate valued at £850,000 and the following bequests:

- £200,000 to his wife
- £100,000 to charity
- The balance to his daughter, including a home valued at £300,000

Calculate:

- The Inheritance Tax payable
- The amount that his daughter will receive

Answers to chapter activities

1 Introduction to Income Tax

1.1 (b) and (e) False; the remaining statements True

1.2 (a) and (d) False; (b), (c) and (e) True

1.3 All the options can provide sources of information about tax law and its interpretation.

1.4

Sample Income	Income Category
UK dividends	Savings and Investment Income
Partnership profits	Trading Income
Rents from land	Property Income
Earnings from a job	Employment, Pension and Social Security Income

1.5 (a), (b) and (c) Receipts basis

1.6 (b), (c), (e) and (f) Exempt; (a) and (d) Not exempt

1.7 (a), (c), (d) and (f) True; (b) and (e) False

1.8 John does not meet the 'automatically resident' test since he was in the UK for less than 183 days, and he has a home outside the UK.

John does not meet the 'automatically not resident' test since he worked in the UK for more than 16 days, and he does not work full-time overseas.

Since John was a UK resident in at least one of the previous three tax years, he needs at least two UK ties to be a UK resident. This is because he spent between 91 and 120 days in the UK.

John has the following UK ties:
- An accommodation tie – his UK flat is always available
- A work tie – he worked more than 40 days in the UK
- A 90 day tie – he spent more than 90 days in the UK in 2022/23, which is one of the two years immediately preceding 2024/25

John is therefore a UK resident in 2024/25.

2 Income from property

2.1

	Two bedroom house £	One bedroom flat £
Income	7,650	6,600
Expenses:		
Management fees	765	
Redecoration	530	
Council Tax & Water		1,100
Insurance		340
Profit	6,355	5,160

2.2

	£	£
Income		12,000
Expenditure:		
Council tax	700	
Water rates	300	
Insurance	380	
Managing agent's charges	1,200	
Replacement furniture	2,100	
		4,680
Assessable Income		7,320

2.3 (a), (c), (d) and (f) Allowable; (b) and (e) Not allowable

2.4 (a), (b), (c), (d) and (f) Allowable; (e) Not allowable

3 Income from savings and investments

3.1 (b) and (c) True; (a) and (d) False

3.2

General Income		£20,070.00	
less personal allowance		£12,570.00	
Taxable		£7,500.00	
Income Tax	£7,500.00 × 20%		£1,500.00
Savings Income		£1,500.00	
Income Tax	£1,000 × 0%		£0.00
	£500 × 20%		£100.00
Dividend Income		£2,000.00	
Income Tax	£500.00 × 0%		£0.00
	£1,500 x 8.75%		£131.25
Total Income Tax			£1,731.25

3.3

General Income	£25,070.00			
less personal allowance	£12,570.00			
Taxable	£12,500.00			
Basic rate	£12,500.00	× 20%		£2,500.00
Savings Income	£3,500.00			
Personal savings allowance:	£1,000.00	× 0%	£0.00	
Basic rate	£2,500.00	× 20%	£500.00	
	£3,500.00			£500.00
Dividend Income	£6,000.00			
Dividend allowance	£500.00	× 0%	£0.00	
Dividend ordinary rate:	£5,500.00	× 8.75%	£481.25	
	£6,000.00			£481.25
Total Income Tax				£3,481.25

3.4

	£	£	£
General Income	60,000.00		
less personal allowance	12,570.00		
Taxable	47,430.00		
£37,700 x 20%		7,540.00	
£9,730 x 40%		3,892.00	
£47,430			11,432.00
Savings Income	7,500.00		
£500 × 0% (Personal savings allowance)		0.00	
£7,000 × 40%		2,800.00	
£7,500			2,800.00
Dividend Income	5,000.00		
£500 × 0% (Dividend allowance)		0.00	
£4,500 × 33.75%		1,518.75	
£5,000			1,518.75
Total Income Tax			15,750.75

3.5 (a), (b), (c), and (e) True; (d) False

4 Income from employment

4.1

Indicators of Employment	Indicators of Self-Employment
Need to do the work yourself	Can employ helper or substitute
Told how, where and when to do work	Decide yourself how, when and where to do work
Work set hours and paid regular wage with sick pay and holidays	Choose work hours and invoice for work done
No risk of capital or losses	Risk own capital and bear losses from work that is not to standard
Employer provides equipment	Provide own equipment
Usually work for one employer	Work for several people or organisations

4.2 (a) (1) 44 g/km 14%
   (2) 134 g/km 31%
   (3) 151 g/km 35%
   (4) 249 g/km 37%

 (b) (1) The cost of the car used in the benefit in kind computation is £17,000

   (2) The percentage used in the benefit in kind computation is 37%

   (3) The assessable benefit for Silvia relating to the car for 2024/25 is £3,145

4.3 (a) (c) £75,000

 (b) (a) and (c) Yes; (b) No

 (c) (c) £8,925   *Workings: (£9,300 + (2.25% × £90,000) – £2,400)*

4.4 £62 *Workings: (£16,000 + £14,000)/2 × 4/12 × (2.25% – 1.0%)*

4.5 (a) (b) She will have a taxable amount of £875
     Workings: (10,000 × (50p – 45p)) + (1,500 × (50p – 25p))

 (b) (b) His taxable salary will be reduced by £1,420
     Workings: (£28,400 × 5%, the employer's contribution is tax-free)

 (c) (b) An allowable deduction of £120 (the net cost to Steve)

 (d) (a) The employer pays a percentage of her salary into the scheme, but Genna does not

5 Preparing Income Tax computations

5.1

	£
Employment Income	57,500
Rental Income	10,350
Savings Income	700
Dividend Income	6,500
less Personal Allowance	12,570
Taxable Income	62,480
Tax Calculation:	
General Income (£57,500 + £10,350 – £12,570) £55,280:	
(£37,700 + £4,000 + £2,000 = £43,700) x 20%	8,740.00
(£55,280 – £43,700) × 40%	4,632.00
Savings Income £700:	
Personal savings allowance £500 x 0%	0.00
(£700 – £500 = £200) × 40%	80.00
Dividend Income £6,500	
Dividend allowance £500 × 0%	0.00
(£6,500 – £500 = £6,000) × 33.75%	2,025.00
Tax liability	15,477.00

5.2

Situation	Dave's tax on savings income £	Sue's tax on savings income £
Current position	200	600
All savings in Dave's name	600	0
All savings in Sue's name	0	1,400

5.3

	Normal situation £	Replacing carpet and curtains £
Taxable Income	45,430	39,430
Tax at 20%	7,540	7,540
Tax at 40%	3,092	692
Total Income Tax	10,632	8,232
Net Cost of Replacements		3,600

5.4

Include any workings:	£
Salary	45,000
Car benefit £22,000 × 33%	7,260
Fuel benefit £27,800 × 33%	9,174
Sub total	61,434
Personal allowance	12,570
Taxable Income	48,864
Tax at 20%: Band £37,700 + (1,600 × 100/80) = £39,700 × 20%	7,940
Tax at 40%: (£48,864 − £39,700) × 40%	3,666
Total tax liability	11,606

5.5

	£
Employment Income	91,500
Dividends	17,500
	109,000
Personal allowance	8,820
Taxable Income	100,180
General Income:	
(37,700 + 1,500) × 20%	7,840
(82,680* − 39,200) × 40%	17,392
Dividend Income:	
500 × 0%	0
17,000 × 33.75%	5,738
Tax liability	30,970

Workings:

Adjusted net income: £91,500 + £17,500 − £1,500 = £107,500

Personal allowance: £12,570 − 50% × (£107,500 − £100,000) = £8,820

*General income: £91,500 − £8,820 = £82,680

6 Capital Gains Tax

6.1

		Actual proceeds used	Deemed proceeds used	No gain or loss basis
(a)	Father gives an asset to his son		✔	
(b)	Wife sells an asset to her husband			✔
(c)	Simon gives an asset to his friend		✔	
(d)	Margaret sells an asset to her cousin for £15,000 when the market value is £40,000	✔		
(e)	Brian gives an asset to his civil partner, Dave			✔

6.2 (c) £4,190

True: legal fees are an allowable deduction where they relate to the purchase or sale of an asset.

6.3 (a), (b) and (d) True; (c) False

6.4 (a) The gain on the asset is £12,500

(b) The amount of loss that will be relieved is £9,500

(c) The Capital Gains Tax payable is £0

(d) The loss to be carried forward to the next tax year is £500

6.5

Asset	Exempt	Chargeable
Antique furniture valued at £30,000		✔
Main private residence	✔	
Clock	✔	
Shares		✔
Holiday home		✔
Government securities	✔	
Vintage car	✔	
Land		✔

6.6 (a)

Occupation / Deemed Occupation	Non-occupation
1/1/2006 – 31/12/2008 (36 months)	
1/1/2009 – 31/12/2009 (12 months)	
1/1/2010 – 30/6/2011 (18 months)	
1/7/2011 – 31/12/2018 (90 months)	1/1/2019 – 31/3/2024 (63 months)
1/4/2024 – 1/1/2025 (9 months)	

(b) Chargeable gain is £22,105 *Workings: ((£205,000 – £125,000) × 63/228)*

6.7

Asset	Sale proceeds	Cost	Statement
1	£4,000	£7,000	Sale proceeds to be £6,000
2	£14,000	£8,000	Calculate gain as normal
3	£8,000	£3,000	Chattel marginal relief applies
4	£3,000	£5,000	Exempt asset
5	£15,000	£21,000	Calculate loss as normal

6.8

	Number of shares	£
October 2000	20,000	100,000
Bonus	800	0
Sub total	20,800	100,000
Disposal	8,000	38,462
Pool balance	12,800	61,538
Proceeds		72,000
Cost		38,462
Gain		33,538

7 Inheritance Tax

7.1

	£
Inheritance Tax calculation:	
Estate	800,000
less exempt transfer to Phil	(250,000)
less exempt transfer to charity	(2,000)
less residence nil rate band	(175,000)
less nil rate band	(325,000)
Amount subject to IHT	48,000
Inheritance Tax at 40%	19,200
Calculation of amount received by Robert:	
Estate	800,000
less transfer to Phil	(250,000)
less transfer to charity	(2,000)
less Inheritance Tax	(19,200)
Balance due to Robert (including home)	528,800

7.2

	£
Mary's estate:	
Estate	350,000
less exempt transfer to Paul (£350,000 − £80,000)	(270,000)
less nil rate band used	(80,000)
Amount subject to IHT	0
Inheritance Tax at 40%	0
Paul's estate:	
Estate	950,000
less residence nil rate band (£175,0000 + £175,000)	(350,000)
less nil rate band (£325,000 + (£325,000 − £80,000))	(570,000)
Chargeable to IHT	30,000
Inheritance Tax at 40%	12,000

7.3

	£	£
Gift to daughter, Rosy	10,000	
less marriage gift exemption	(5,000)	
		(5,000)
less current year annual exemption		(3,000)
less part of prior year annual exemption		(2,000)
The gift to Rosy does not result in PET		0
Gift to son, Robert		5,000
less balance of prior year annual exemption		(1,000)
PET resulting from gift to Robert		4,000
PET resulting from gift to parents (no deductions)		2,500

The gifts to charity, the Labour Party, and her husband are all exempt transfers.

7.4 Inheritance Tax due in lifetime:

The chargeable transfer will not result in any IHT payable immediately, since (after deducting two £3,000 annual exemptions) it is £164,000, which is below the £325,000 threshold.

The gift to David is a PET of £20,000, less annual exemption of £3,000 = £17,000. The gift to Masie is a PET of £30,000.

Inheritance Tax on death:

	£
Estate	630,000
less exempt transfer to wife, Julie	(250,000)
less exempt transfer to charity	(5,000)
less nil rate band	
(£325,000 – £164,000 – £17,000 – £30,000)	(114,000)
Chargeable to IHT	261,000
Inheritance Tax at 40%	104,400

7.5

	£
Inheritance Tax calculation	
Estate	850,000
less exempt transfer to Jim's wife	(200,000)
less exempt transfer to charity	(100,000)
less residence nil rate band	(175,000)
less nil rate band	(325,000)
Amount subject to IHT	50,000
Inheritance Tax at 36%*	18,000

*The 'net value' of the estate is (£850,000 – £200,000 – £175,000 – £325,000) = £150,000. The payment to charity of £100,000 is equal to more than 10% of £150,000, and so the rate of 36% applies.

Calculation of amount received by Jim's daughter:

	£
Estate	850,000
less exempt transfer to Jim's wife	(200,000)
less exempt transfer to charity	(100,000)
less Inheritance Tax	(18,000)
Balance due to Jim's daughter (including home)	532,000

Practice assessment 1

Task 1

(a) You work for a small firm of accountants. One of your clients has arrived for a meeting to review the accounts and tax work that you have completed for his small business. The business's taxable profits are typically about £70,000 per year, and this year's figures show a similar profit.

The client looks at the figures, and then states 'I don't want to provide HMRC with such a high profit figure. I would like to show profits at nearer £50,000 so that I can avoid the higher rate of tax. I don't mind how you adjust the figures – after all it's just a bit of harmless tax avoidance that everyone does.'

Explain how you will deal with this situation.

(b) David is single, with no children. He is employed and currently works both in the UK and France. He has a house in the UK which is always available, and he uses it when he is in the country. He also has a flat in France where he lives when he is working there.

He was not a UK resident in 2022/23, but he was a UK resident in 2023/24 (when he spent 95 days working in the UK).

In 2024/25 David spent 165 days in the UK working. He spent the rest of the year in France.

Using the appropriate tests, explain whether David is a UK resident for 2024/25.

Task 2

(a) Joe had two company cars during 2024/25 and his employer paid the running costs of each car, including all fuel. The following table shows the details.

Car	Number of months	List price £	Price paid £	Joe's capital contribution £	Scale charge %
Ford	4	25,350	25,150	1,000	23
Fiat	8	31,250	22,500	6,500	19

Complete the following table to show Joe's taxable benefit in kind for the cars for 2024/25. Show your answers to the nearest £.

	£
The benefit in kind for the use of the Ford car	
The benefit in kind for the provision of fuel for the Ford car	
The benefit in kind for the use of the Fiat car	
The benefit in kind for the provision of fuel for the Fiat car	

(b) Complete the following table by inserting the scale charge for 2024/25 for each of the cars shown.

	Engine type	CO_2 emissions	Scale charge %
Car 1	Diesel (not RDE2 compliant)	145	
Car 2	Petrol – electric hybrid Electric only range 33 miles	44	

(c) The following table shows a list of benefits relating to employment. Enter the assessable amount (or zero for any that are exempt) for each benefit. Round answers down to £ if necessary.

	Assessable Amount £
Private use of a small van including private fuel from 1 September 2024 until 31 December 2024	
An interest-free loan of £9,000, repayable over two years from the loan date of 1 June 2024	
Use of a company flat with an annual value of £5,000. The flat was bought in 2012 for £130,000, and was valued at £200,000 when first occupied by this employee. The flat is not job-related	
Use of a home cinema system bought by the employer for £2,000 for the employee's use from 6 June 2024	
A holiday costing £500 was paid for using a company credit card (with the employer's permission)	
Free workplace parking in a public car park that costs the employer £2,860 per year	

Task 3

(a) Complete the following sentence for each taxpayer. Enter answers in whole pounds only.

Mabel received a dividend of £7,400. Her other income, after the personal allowance, was £32,000.

The tax payable on the dividends is £ [_____]

John received £1,650 interest from his bank and £560 interest from his individual savings account. His other taxable income, after the personal allowance, was £63,500.

The tax payable on savings income is £ [_____]

Vikram received building society interest income of £4,400. His other income was £161,500.

The tax payable on savings income is £ [_____]

(b) Complete the following table to show the taxable rent and the allowable expenses for each property. Enter amounts in whole pounds only. All properties are owned by the same individual.

Property	Details	Taxable rent £	Allowable expenses £
10 Major Road	This property was first let on 1 December in the tax year for £800 per month. The tenant paid six months' rent in advance, plus a refundable deposit of £1,000. The landlord paid £65 property insurance per month.		
2 Little Lane	This property was let all the tax year for £1,200 per month. The managing agent charged 12% of the rent received. The bathroom fittings were replaced costing £1,500.		
4 Manor Park	This property was occupied by the landlord's son until 30 June in the tax year. The interior was then repainted, costing £800, and a tenant moved in on 6 July, paying £900 per month. A washing machine was purchased for the property in July costing £550. There had not been one in the property previously.		

(c) Identify whether the following statements are true or false.

Statement	True	False
An additional rate taxpayer is entitled to up to £500 savings allowance, but no dividend allowance		
The cost of tidying up an overgrown garden between tenancies is an allowable property expense		

Task 4

Nigel has the following income for the tax year:

Income from employment	£49,500
Property Income	£10,350
Bank interest received	£1,380
Dividends received	£6,400

Nigel has property income losses brought forward of £2,100.

During the tax year, Nigel made gifts to charities under gift-aid of £1,840.

Using the blank table below, calculate Nigel's total Income Tax liability. Round amounts to the £ below.

Task 5

(a) During the tax year, Celia received a gross salary of £53,500 and use of a company car with an assessable benefit value of £6,150.

Complete the following table to show the National Insurance Contributions relating to Celia in whole pounds. Ignore the employment allowance.

	£
The total Class 1 NIC payable by Celia in the tax year	
The total Class 1 NIC payable by Celia's employer in the tax year	
The total Class 1A NIC payable by Celia's employer relating to the tax year	

(b) Identify whether the following statements are true or false.

Statement	True	False
Employees' National Insurance Contributions are calculated on a cumulative basis throughout the tax year for all employees		
Class 1A NIC is payable by both employees and employers on benefits in kind		

Task 6

(a) Indicate with ticks whether each of the following statements is true or false.

		True	False
(a)	For an interest-free personal loan from an employer to be an exempt benefit, the total loan(s) must not exceed £10,000 during the tax year		
(b)	A transfer of money to a husband, wife, or civil partner has no implications for either Capital Gains Tax or Inheritance Tax		

(b) Complete the sentences below.

Dick and Jane are married. They have £60,000 to invest in a savings account that pays 4% interest per year. They have no other savings income. Dick's employment income is £21,000 per year, and Jane's employment income is £63,000 per year.

If the £60,000 is invested in a savings account in Dick's name, the tax payable will be

£ _____ less than if it is invested in Jane's name.

Julie has total income of £110,000 per year. If she pays £4,000 (net) to a charity under gift aid, her personal allowance will increase by £ _____ .

Rashid will have use of a diesel company car (not RDE2 compliant) for the whole tax year with a list price of £30,000, and car benefit of 25%. He is a higher rate taxpayer. If Rashid changes this car to a petrol model of the same age, and with the same list price, but a CO_2 figure 10 g/km lower, it would save him

£ _____ per year in tax (excluding fuel benefit).

Task 7

(a) For each statement, tick the appropriate box.

		Actual proceeds used	Deemed proceeds used	No gain or loss basis
(1)	Dave gives an asset to his father			
(2)	Peter sells an asset to his friend			
(3)	Simon gives an asset to his friend			

(b) John has a capital loss brought forward of £2,500. He has taxable income for the year of £25,000.

He sold an asset during the tax year for £23,000 (not residential property). He had been left the asset when his grandfather died. His grandfather had paid £6,000 for the asset, and it was valued at £9,500 at the time of death.

Complete the following sentences:

(1) The gain on the asset is £ ☐

(2) The amount of loss that will be relieved is £ ☐

(3) The Capital Gains Tax payable is £ ☐

(4) The loss to be carried forward to the next tax year is £ ☐

(c) Complete the following table to show which assets are exempt from Capital Gains Tax and which are chargeable.

Asset	Exempt	Chargeable
Land		✓
Main private residence	✓	
Antique painting valued at £20,000		✓
Unquoted shares		✓
Caravan	✓	
Government securities	✓	
Classic car	✓	
Horse	✓	

Task 8

Pam bought 25,000 shares in Lester Ltd for £5 per share in October 2000. In April 2005 she took up a rights issue of 3 for 5 at £4 per share. In January 2025, Pam sold 10,000 shares for £8 per share.

Clearly showing the balance of shares, and their value to carry forward, calculate the gain made on these shares. All workings must be shown in your calculations.

Task 9

(a) The following information is available about four taxpayers who sold capital assets (not residential property) during the tax year. These were their only capital asset disposals. Complete the table to show the Capital Gains Tax payable by each individual, in whole pounds.

Taxpayer	Sold to	Proceeds £	Market value £	Cost £	Other taxable income £	Capital Gains Tax £
Dave	Son	31,500	40,000	25,000	48,000	
Brian	Wife	10,000	50,000	45,000	63,000	
Sue	Friend	15,000	18,000	14,000	21,000	
Alison	Friend	33,000	25,000	13,500	33,000	

(b) Sophie bought her flat on 1 January 2013 for £120,000, and immediately used it as her only residence. In April 2018 she went on an extended holiday for 8 months, and let a friend stay in the flat until she returned.

Sophie bought a house on 1 July 2023, and immediately used it as her only residence. The expected sale of the flat was delayed until 31 December 2024, when it was eventually sold for £192,000.

Calculate the amount of her gain that will be subject to CGT before deducting the annual exempt amount.

£ ☐

Task 10

(a) The following lifetime transfers were made by unconnected individuals. Complete the table to show the value of any potentially exempt transfers, assuming that the annual exempt amounts for the current and previous year have already been utilised. If any transfers are wholly exempt enter a zero.

	Value of PET £
Gill gives Dave £5,000 to celebrate their forthcoming marriage	4,000
Roger donates £10,000 to the National Trust (a registered charity)	0
Sue gives her daughter £10,000 to help with a house deposit	10,000

(b) Analyse the following statements about Inheritance Tax into those that are true and those that are false.

		True	False
(a)	Individuals that are not domiciled in the UK are always liable for IHT on transfers of their worldwide property		✓
(b)	Individuals that are resident and domiciled in the UK are liable for IHT on transfers of their worldwide property	✓	
(c)	A donation to a qualifying political party is an exempt transfer whether made during the individual's lifetime or on death	✓	

(c) Harry and Sue were married. When Harry died in 2022, he utilised all his nil rate band and half of his residence nil rate band.

Sue died in 2024. She left all her estate valued at £900,000, including a home valued at £500,000, to her daughter. She had made no lifetime transfers

Calculate the total amount of nil rate band and residence nil rate band that can be deducted in the calculation of IHT on Sue's estate.

£ 587,500

Practice assessment 2

Task 1

(a) You work for a small firm of accountants. One of your clients is self employed in the entertainment industry, and an additional rate taxpayer. She has arrived for a meeting that she requested.

She explains that she has been introduced to a 'tax minimisation specialist' who has recommended that she joins a tax avoidance scheme. The scheme involves using various offshore companies which can divert her earnings through a complicated system. She understands that this will save her 'a substantial amount of tax'. She has also been told that HMRC is 'aware of the scheme'.

The client is keen to go ahead, and asks you to explain the differences between tax avoidance and tax evasion, and any implications of joining the scheme.

Give your response in the box below, and note briefly the ethical implications.

(b) Two ways that taxes can be categorised are progressive and regressive. Explain each of these terms, and then give an example of a tax that is progressive and of a tax that is regressive.

Task 2

(a) Miranda had the use of two company cars during the tax year. The company paid for all the running costs of the cars, including all fuel.

Details of the cars are as follows:

Car	Period of use	List price £	Cost £	CO_2 emissions	Type of engine
Ford	5 months of the tax year	28,500	27,600	139 g/km	Petrol
Citroen	7 months of the tax year	29,060	29,000	85 g/km	Diesel (RDE2 compliant)

Complete the following table to show Miranda's taxable benefit in kind for the cars for the tax year. Show amounts to the nearest £.

Car		%	£
Ford	Scale charge percentage		
	Taxable benefit on provision of the car		
	Taxable benefit on provision of fuel		
Citroen	Scale charge percentage		
	Taxable benefit on provision of the car		
	Taxable benefit on provision of fuel		
Total taxable benefit			

(b) Complete the following table by inserting the scale charge for 2024/25 for each of the cars shown.

	Engine type	CO_2 emissions	Scale charge %
Car 1	Petrol	143	
Car 2	Electric	0	

(c) Indicate whether each of the following will or will not result in an assessable benefit in kind for the employee by ticking the appropriate box.

The following are provided by the employer to the employee		Assessable benefit in kind	Not assessable benefit in kind
(a)	Subscription to gym that is also used by non-employees	✓	
(b)	Allowance of £5 per night for incidental costs while staying away from home on business		✓
(c)	Relocation costs of £5,000 when required to move house by the employer		✓

(d) Robert was provided with the following by his employer during the tax year:

- A new computer games console to use at home for the whole tax year. This cost the employer £350, and remains the employer's property. By the end of the tax year the console was valued at £100.

- An interest-free loan of £14,000 at the start of the tax year. Robert repaid £6,000 on 6 January 2025, but made no other repayments.

- Mileage allowance of 60p per mile for business journeys using Robert's own car. Robert claimed for trips totalling 13,000 miles.

Complete the following table to show the total assessable benefits (if any). Round amounts down to £ if necessary.

	Assessable amount £
Use of computer games console	
Interest-free loan	
Mileage allowance	

Task 3

(a) Complete the following sentence for each taxpayer. Enter answers in whole pounds only.

Mary received a dividend of £6,200. Her other income, before personal allowances, was £21,500.

The tax payable on the dividends is £ ☐

Joe received £650 interest from his bank and £1,560 interest from his individual savings account. His other taxable income, after the personal allowance was £46,500.

The tax payable on savings income is £ ☐

Alex received dividend income of £4,150. His other income was £152,500.

The tax payable on dividend income is £ ☐

(b) Complete the following table to show the taxable rent and the allowable expenses for each property. Enter amounts in whole pounds only. Rent is normally received on the 1st of each month.

Property	Details	Taxable rent £	Allowable expenses £
12 Water Road	This property was let for the whole tax year for £900 per month. The landlord paid £85 per month property insurance. The property flooded in December. The insurance company paid £4,000 out of the £4,500 cost of repairs.		
Upper Lodge	This property was let until 30 June for £1,200 per month. The property was then empty until 1 August, when it was let for the rest of the tax year at £1,250 per month. The managing agent charged 12% of the rent received. The carpets were replaced, costing £1,200, during July.		
Manor House	This property was let out until 31 January in the tax year at £1,800 per month. The tenant moved out, owing rent for December and January, and cannot be located. The interior was then repainted costing £1,700 and a new tenant moved in on 6 April. Insurance costs were £60 per month throughout the tax year.		

(c) Identify whether the following statements are true or false.

Statement	True	False
The savings allowance can be set against dividend income where the individual has no savings income		
The cost of insuring a property during a period in between tenancies is an allowable property expense		

Task 4

Sadiq has the following income for the tax year:

Income from employment	£97,500
Property Income	£6,060
Bank interest received	£780
Dividends received	£5,200

Sadiq has property income losses brought forward of £8,100.

During the tax year, Sadiq made net payments into a personal pension scheme of £2,000.

Using the blank table below, calculate Sadiq's total Income Tax liability. Show amounts in whole £s.

Task 5

(a) During the tax year, Donna received a gross salary of £43,900 and benefits in kind with an assessable value of £10,400.

Complete the following table to show the National Insurance Contributions relating to Donna in whole pounds. Ignore the employment allowance.

	£
The total Class 1 NIC payable by Donna in the tax year	
The total Class 1 NIC payable by Donna's employer in the tax year	
The total Class 1A NIC payable by Donna's employer relating to the tax year	

(b) Identify whether the following statements are true or false.

Statement	True	False
Employees' National Insurance Contributions are the same amounts for employees of all ages		
The employment allowance can be set against both employers' and employees' NIC		

Task 6

(a) Indicate with ticks whether each of the following statements is true or false.

		True	False
(a)	For a personal loan from an employer to be an assessable benefit, the total loan(s) must exceed £10,000 during the tax year and the interest rate must be lower than the official rate		
(b)	When an individual transfers their cash ISA to a different provider, they lose the tax-free status of the interest for the current tax year		

(b) Complete the sentences below.

Paul and Cath are married. They are considering buying 20,000 shares in a company that consistently pays dividends of 40 pence per share each year. Paul's employment income is £32,000 per year, and Cath's employment income is £58,000 per year. They have no other income.

If the shares are bought in Paul's name, the tax payable on the dividends will be

£ _____ less than if they are bought in Cath's name.

Joan has total income of £110,000 per year, including provisional property income of £20,000. She does not claim the property allowance.

If Joan spends an extra £3,000 replacing a carpet in a rental property, she will save tax of £ [   ].

Roger will have use of a diesel company car (not RDE2) for the whole tax year, together with free fuel. The car benefit is 35%. He is a higher rate taxpayer. If Roger changes this car to a petrol model with a CO_2 figure 35 g/km lower, it would save him annual tax on just the fuel benefit of £ [   ] to the nearest £.

Task 7

(a) Indicate whether each of the following statements is true or false.

		True	False
(a)	A chattel bought and sold for less than £6,000 is exempt from Capital Gains Tax		
(b)	Transfers between spouses are carried out on a 'no gain, no loss' basis		
(c)	Capital Gains Tax will be incurred on the increase in value of investments between the date of purchase and the date of the owner's death		
(d)	Mechanical chattels (for example clocks) owned for personal use are exempt from Capital Gains Tax		

(b) Josie bought a painting for £14,000 and spent £3,000 having it restored and £800 insuring it. She sold it for £16,000.

Select the capital gain or loss on disposal from the following:

(a)	Zero (exempt asset)	
(b)	Gain of £2,000	
(c)	Loss of £1,000	
(d)	Loss of £1,800	

(c) Jack's grandfather, John, bought an asset for £6,600. Some years later John died and left the asset to Jack in his will. The asset was valued at £9,400 at that time.

Recently, Jack sold the asset to his sister, Jill, for £6,000 when it was valued at £11,000.

Complete the following table to calculate the gain or loss when Jack sold the asset to Jill. Use a minus sign to denote a loss.

	£
Proceeds or deemed proceeds	
Cost or deemed cost	
Gain or loss	

Task 8

Ken bought 800 shares in Kandle Ltd for £3,000 in April 2003. In May 2009 he bought a further 1,200 shares for £3.90 each. In December 2010 a rights issue of 1 for 5 at £2.00 per share was offered, and Ken took up the offer.

Ken sold 500 shares on 11 November 2024 for a total of £3,000. On 23 December 2024 he purchased a further 100 shares for £6.30 each.

Clearly showing the balance of shares and their value to carry forward, calculate the gain made on the sale of shares that occurred in 2024/25.

Task 9

(a) The following information is available about four taxpayers who sold capital assets (not residential property) during the tax year. These were their only capital asset disposals. Complete the table to show the Capital Gains Tax payable by each individual, in whole pounds.

Taxpayer	Sold to	Proceeds £	Market value £	Cost £	Other taxable income £	Capital Gains Tax £
Adam	Cousin	41,500	50,000	29,000	58,000	3,600
Ben	Wife	35,000	40,000	20,000	23,000	0
Chloe	Stranger	25,000	28,000	12,000	21,000	1,000
Della	Friend	23,000	35,000	10,500	31,000	950

(b) Angela had the following capital gains and losses in the last few years.

Year	Annual exempt amount £	Capital gains £	Capital Losses £
2022/23	12,300	20,100	28,450
2023/24	6,000	13,400	2,600
2024/25	3,000	18,400	2,150

Complete the following table, using '0' if any answer is zero:

The amount chargeable to CGT in 2024/25 is	£ 9,700
The capital loss to be carried forward to 2025/26 is	£ 0

Task 10

(a) The following lifetime transfers were the only gifts made in the tax year by unconnected individuals. Complete the table to show the value of any potentially exempt transfers, assuming that the annual exempt amounts for the current and previous year have not been utilised. If any transfers are wholly exempt, enter a zero.

	Value of PET £
Sue gives her daughter £12,000 to celebrate her marriage	
Roger donates £20,000 to a qualifying political party	0
Richard gives his son £25,000 to help with a house deposit	19,000

(b) Analyse the following statements about Inheritance Tax into those that are true and those that are false.

		True	False
(a)	The annual allowance of £3,000 can be used as a deduction from a death estate		✓
(b)	Taper relief can reduce the tax rate at death where lifetime transfers were made between three and seven years before death	✓	
(c)	When any amount is bequeathed to charity at death, the tax rate on the chargeable part of the estate is reduced to 36%		✓

(c) The only lifetime transfer made by Helen was a PET of £400,000 (after exemptions) made on 31 December 2018.

Helen died on 31 January 2025.

Complete the following:

The amount of the PET that is now chargeable to Inheritance Tax is £ _____

The amount of Inheritance Tax payable on the PET is £ _____

The Inheritance Tax is payable by [select option] _____

Options: the executor of Helen's estate

the recipient of the PET

Practice assessment 3

Task 1

(a) Explain the terms domicile and residence, and briefly discuss how an individual's domicile and residence is determined.

Outline the tax implications for an individual who is UK resident, but not UK domiciled.

(b) Caroline had been a UK resident all her life. She decided to leave the UK to go on a gap year, and she left on 1 September 2024. She gave up her rented apartment and her job on that date, and planned to travel, staying in hostels or camping. Caroline is single, with no children. She had lived and worked in the UK for 148 days in 2024/25.

Explain, using appropriate rules, whether Caroline is a UK resident for 2024/25.

Task 2

(a) Dirk is a senior manager in the defence industry. During the tax year he was provided with the following company cars:

From the start of the tax year until 30 June he was provided with a Jaguar. It was purchased for £41,000 secondhand, and had a list price of £52,000. Its emissions were 152 g/km and it was powered by a petrol engine.

Following a promotion for Dirk, the Jaguar was replaced with a new diesel-powered Range Rover, registered and provided on 1 July. This car had a list price of £72,000. The company believed that Dirk's new role placed him at increased risk of a terrorism attack, and paid £25,000 for the Range Rover to be equipped with bullet resistant glass and strengthened bodywork. The emissions of the car were 230 g/km. The car complies with RDE2.

On 1 December the car was fitted with passengers' televisions so that Dirk's family could be entertained on long trips. This cost the company £1,200.

Complete the following table to show the benefit in kind arising from the use of these cars. Ignore any benefit arising from private fuel.

Car	Percentage applicable based on CO_2 emissions %	Cost of car used in benefit calculation £	Benefit in kind £
Jaguar			
Range Rover			
Total			

(b) Complete the following table by inserting the scale charge for 2024/25 for each of the cars shown.

	Engine type	CO_2 emissions	Scale charge %
Car 1	Diesel RDE2 compliant	142	
Car 2	Petrol hybrid (electric range 45 miles)	25	

(c) Place a tick in the appropriate column of the table below to show whether each of the items listed would or would not result in an assessable benefit in kind for an employee.

The following are provided by the employer to the employee		Benefit in kind	No benefit in kind
(a)	Use of a company credit card to pay for the entertainment of customers (with approval of the employer)		✓
(b)	Mileage payment for use of employee's own motorcycle for business purposes at a rate of 24p per mile		✓
(c)	Petrol for travel from home to work in a company car	✓	
(d)	Training costs including course and examination fees for accountancy trainee undertaking AAT course		✓

(d) Calculate the assessable benefit in kind (in whole pounds) for each of the following:

	Benefit £
On 6 April an employee was provided with an interest-free loan of £15,000. During the tax year he made three repayments, each of £2,000. The remainder of the loan was still outstanding at the end of the tax year.	
On 6 April an employee was allowed the use of a home cinema system that had previously been used by the company. The home cinema had originally cost the company £1,500, but its market value on 6 April was £1,000.	

Task 3

(a) Complete the following sentence for each taxpayer. Enter answers in whole pounds only.

Monica received a dividend of £6,000. Her other income was £151,500.

The tax payable on the dividends is £ [ ]

Jonathan received £2,650 interest from his bank. His only other income was employment income of £24,000.

The tax payable on savings income is £ [ ]

Alan received dividend income of £6,200. His other income, before the personal allowance, was £52,500.

The tax payable on dividend income is £ [ ]

(b) Complete the following table to show the taxable rent and the allowable expenses (or property allowance if applicable) for each property/landlord. Enter amounts in whole pounds only. Each property is let by a separate individual landlord.

Property	Details	Taxable rent £	Allowable expenses/ Property allowance £
1 Henry Road	This property was let for the whole tax year for £950 per month. The landlord paid £40 per month property insurance. During the year, the landlord installed central heating where none existed previously, costing £6,000.		
Middle House	This property was let until 5 October for £1,000 per month. The property was then used as a second home by the landlord. The buildings insurance was £20 per month.		
3 Lincoln Road	This property was let out until 5 February in the tax year at £800 per month. The interior was then decorated costing £1,200, and the carpets were replaced costing £1,800. A new tenant moved in on 6 March paying £820 per month.		

(c) Identify whether the following statements are true or false.

Statement	True	False
The adjusted net income can be used to help determine the level of personal savings allowance that is available in complex situations		
The cost of renovating a property to bring it up to a suitable standard before it is first let out is not an allowable property expense		

Task 4

Sarah has the following income for the tax year:

Income from employment	£45,000
Property Income	£8,150
Bank interest received	£1,780
Dividends received	£4,200

During the tax year, Sarah made net payments into a personal pension scheme of £800.

Using the blank table below, calculate Sarah's total Income Tax liability (in whole £s).

Task 5

(a) During the tax year, Ellen received a gross salary of £12,000 and benefits in kind with an assessable value of £400.

Complete the following table to show the National Insurance Contributions relating to Ellen in whole pounds. Ignore the employment allowance.

	£
The total Class 1 NIC payable by Ellen in the tax year	0
The total Class 1 NIC payable by Ellen's employer in the tax year	400
The total Class 1A NIC payable by Ellen's employer relating to the tax year	55

(b) Identify whether the following statements are true or false.

Statement	True	False
A cumulative income calculation is carried out to check that NIC for directors is not distorted by unusual payment patterns	✓	
Where total employers' NIC for an organisation is below £5,000, then HMRC will pay the difference between that figure and £5,000 to the organisation		✓

Task 6

(a) Indicate with ticks whether each of the following statements is true or false.

		True	False
(a)	If a wholly electric car is provided as a company car, the benefit percentage will be 2% for use of the car, and any electricity charging provided by the employer will be tax-free	✓	
(b)	Individuals aged 18 or over can move their investment from a cash ISA to a stocks and shares ISA without any restrictions	✓	

(b) Complete the sentences below.

Peter is a basic rate taxpayer in the current year, but will be a higher rate taxpayer next year. He currently has no savings income, but has recently been given £50,000 from his late uncle's estate. He is considering a one year savings account that has two options for receiving interest. A monthly interest option would give him interest of £400 this tax year and £600 next tax year. An annual interest option would mean that he receives £1,000 next tax year.

If the monthly interest option is chosen, then over the two tax years Peter will pay

£ 160   less tax on savings income than if the annual interest option is chosen.

Jo has total income of £106,000 per year. If Jo earned a further £1,000 as an employment bonus, her tax would increase by £ _____ .

Roland is a basic rate taxpayer. His employer has offered a scheme in which Roland's pay would reduce by £40 per week, but the company would increase its pension contributions by the same amount.

In a full tax year, this would save Roland Income Tax of £ _____ .

Task 7

(a) A taxpayer had previously bought an asset for £14,000, plus 6% auction commission. He sold it during the tax year for £15,000, having spent £100 to advertise it for sale. The cost of insuring the asset during his ownership was £150.

Calculate the gain or loss using the following computation.

	Amount £
Proceeds	14,900
Total costs	14,840
Gain / Loss	60

(b) Complete the following table to show which statements are true and which are false in connection with Capital Gains Tax.

Statement		True	False
(a)	Gifts to charities are exempt from Capital Gains Tax	✓	
(b)	Gifts between a father and son are exempt from Capital Gains Tax		✓
(c)	When applying the 5/3 restriction to chattels, the proceeds figure used is before any costs of sale are deducted	✓	
(d)	Chattels are defined as tangible moveable property	✓	
(e)	Non-wasting chattels are exempt from Capital Gains Tax		✓

(c) Complete the following sentences.

A taxpayer had capital losses brought forward of £9,000. During the tax year he made two disposals, making a gain of £16,300 on one and a loss of £1,900 on the other.

The amount subject to Capital Gains Tax for the year (after the annual exempt amount) will be:

£ 0

The capital loss to be carried forward to be set against future gains will be:

£ 6,900

Task 8

Paul bought 18,000 shares in Leicester Ltd for £4.50 per share in October 2000. In April 2012, he took up a rights issue of 4 for 9 at £3 per share. In January 2025, Paul sold 12,000 shares for £6 per share.

Clearly showing the balance of shares, and their value to carry forward, calculate the gain made on these shares. All workings must be shown in your calculations.

Task 9

(a) The following information is available about four taxpayers who sold capital assets (not residential property) during the tax year. These were their only capital asset disposals. Complete the table to show the Capital Gains Tax payable by each individual, in whole pounds.

Taxpayer	Sold to	Proceeds £	Market value £	Cost £	Other taxable income £	Capital Gains Tax £
Ella	Grandfather	48,500	55,000	24,000	58,000	
Fred	Civil Partner	29,000	40,000	12,000	20,000	
Gareth	Stranger	25,000	20,000	10,000	22,000	
Helen	Friend	20,000	32,000	8,500	45,000	

(b) Mike had the following capital gains and losses in the last few years.

Year	Annual exempt amount £	Capital gains £	Capital Losses £
2022/23	12,300	18,300	7,140
2023/24	6,000	10,400	12,150
2024/25	3,000	17,450	1,150

Complete the following table, using '0' if any answer is zero:

The amount chargeable to CGT in 2024/25 is	£ 11550
The capital loss to be carried forward to 2025/26 is	£

Task 10

(a) The following lifetime transfers were the only gifts made in the tax year by unconnected individuals. Complete the table to show the value of any potentially exempt transfers, assuming that the annual exempt amounts for the current and previous year have not been utilised. If any transfers are wholly exempt enter a zero.

	Value of PET £
Stan gives his son £15,000 to celebrate his marriage	
Ron donates £2,000 to a museum	
Robert gives his nephew £15,000 to help with a house deposit	

(b) Analyse the following statements about Inheritance Tax into those that are true and those that are false.

		True	False
(a)	The annual allowance of £3,000 can only be carried forward for one tax year		
(b)	Taper relief can reduce the tax rate at death where lifetime transfers were made between zero and three years before death		
(c)	When more than 10% of the net value of an estate is bequeathed to charity at death, the tax rate on the chargeable part of the estate is reduced to 36%		

(c) Michelle (who was single) made the following potentially exempt transfers (after exemptions):

25 December 2016   £150,000

31 January 2023   £150,000

Michelle died on 15 February 2025, leaving an estate valued at £400,000, which was left as follows:

£350,000 to her friend

£50,000 to charity.

The nil rate band available at death will be £ ☐

The rate of Inheritance Tax charged on the relevant part of the death estate will be: ☐ %

The Inheritance Tax payable due to Michelle's death must be paid by the following date: ☐

Answers to practice assessment 1

Task 1

(a) The accounts and tax work that have already been undertaken should be reviewed with the client to ensure that all allowances have been accounted for in the most tax-efficient manner. This is normal tax minimisation.

What the client is proposing is illegal tax evasion, not legal tax avoidance. The suggestion is that the accounts are manipulated to reduce the amount of tax that appears to be due. Tax evasion is a criminal activity.

The AAT Code of Professional Ethics makes it clear that accountancy and tax work must be carried out with professional competence and be consistent with the law. To 'adjust' the figures in the way suggested would not be consistent with the law, and must not be carried out.

Although the client would bear ultimate responsibility for submissions made to HMRC, we cannot be associated with any submission that we believe contains inaccuracies.

The client should be asked to reconsider his request that we alter the figures, and asked to agree to submit the original data. If he refuses then we should cease to act for him.

We would then inform HMRC that we no longer act for the client. The reason for ceasing to act would not normally be given to HMRC, as this would be a breach of confidentiality. There appears to be no suggestion here of money laundering which could override the rules regarding confidentiality.

(b) David does not meet the 'automatically resident' test since he was in the UK for less than 183 days, and he has a home outside the UK.

David does not meet the 'automatically not resident' test since he worked in the UK for more than 16 days, and he does not work full-time overseas.

Since David was a UK resident in at least one of the previous three tax years, he needs at least one UK tie to be a UK resident. This is because he spent over 120 days in the UK.

David has the following UK ties:

- An accommodation tie – his UK house that is always available
- A work tie – he worked more than 40 days in the UK
- A 90 day tie – he spent more than 90 days in the UK in 2023/24, which is one of the two years immediately preceding 2024/25

David is therefore a UK resident in 2024/25.

Task 2

(a)

	£
The benefit in kind for the use of the Ford car	1,867
The benefit in kind for the provision of fuel for the Ford car	2,131
The benefit in kind for the use of the Fiat car	3,325
The benefit in kind for the provision of fuel for the Fiat car	3,521

(b)

	Engine type	CO_2 emissions	Scale charge %
Car 1	Diesel (not RDE2 compliant)	145	37
Car 2	Petrol – electric hybrid Electric only range 33 miles	44	12

(c)

	Assessable amount £
Private use of a small van including private fuel from 1 September 2024 until 31 December 2024	1,572
An interest-free loan of £9,000, repayable over two years from the loan date of 1 June 2024	0
Use of a company flat with an annual value of £5,000. The flat was bought in 2012 for £130,000, and was valued at £200,000 when first occupied by this employee. The flat is not job-related	7,812
Use of a home cinema system bought by the employer for £2,000 for the employee's use from 6 June 2024	333
A holiday costing £500 was paid for using a company credit card (with the employer's permission)	500
Free workplace parking in a public car park that costs the employer £2,860 per year	0

Task 3

(a) The tax payable on the dividends is **£1,028**

The tax payable on savings income is **£460**

The tax payable on savings income is **£1,980**

(b)

Property	Taxable rent £	Allowable expenses £
10 Major Road	4,800	260
2 Little Lane	14,400	3,228
4 Manor Park	8,100	800

(c)

Statement	True	False
An additional rate taxpayer is entitled to up to £500 savings allowance, but no dividend allowance		✔
The cost of tidying up an overgrown garden between tenancies is an allowable property expense	✔	

Task 4

	Workings	£
Employment Income		49,500
Property Income	£10,350 – £2,100	8,250
Savings Income		1,380
Dividend Income		6,400
less personal allowance		12,570
Taxable Income		52,960
General Income £45,180	£49,500 + £8,250 – £12,570	
Tax on General Income:	(£37,700 + (£1,840/0.8)) × 20%	8,000
	£5,180 × 40%	2,072
Tax on Savings Income:	£500 × 0%	0
	£880 × 40%	352
Tax on Dividend Income:	£500 × 0%	0
	£5,900 × 33.75%	1,991
Tax liability		12,415

Task 5

(a)

	£
The total Class 1 NIC payable by Celia in the tax year	3,080
The total Class 1 NIC payable by Celia's employer in the tax year	6,127
The total Class 1A NIC payable by Celia's employer relating to the tax year	848

(b)

Statement	True	False
Employees' national insurance contributions are calculated on a cumulative basis throughout the tax year for all employees		✔
Class 1A NIC is payable by both employees and employers on benefits in kind		✔

Task 6

(a) Both are True

(b) If the £60,000 is invested in a savings account in Dick's name, the tax payable will be **£480** less than if it is invested in Jane's name.

Julie has total income of £110,000 per year. If she pays £4,000 (net) to a charity under gift aid, her personal allowance will increase by **£2,500**.

If Rashid changes this car to a petrol model of the same age, and with the same list price, but a CO_2 figure 10 g/km lower, it would save him **£720** per year in tax (excluding fuel benefit).

Task 7

(a)

		Actual proceeds used	Deemed proceeds used	No gain or loss basis
(1)	Dave gives an asset to his father		✔	
(2)	Peter sells an asset to his friend	✔		
(3)	Simon gives an asset to his friend		✔	

(b)
(1) The gain on the asset is **£13,500**

(2) The amount of loss that will be relieved is **£2,500**

(3) The Capital Gains Tax payable is **£800**

(4) The loss to be carried forward to the next tax year is **£0**

(c)

Asset	Exempt	Chargeable
Land		✔
Main private residence	✔	
Antique painting valued at £20,000		✔
Unquoted shares		✔
Caravan	✔	
Government securities	✔	
Classic car	✔	
Horse	✔	

Task 8

	Number of Shares	Value £
Purchase	25,000	125,000
Rights	15,000	60,000
Sub total	40,000	185,000
Disposal	10,000	46,250
Balance	30,000	138,750
Proceeds		80,000
Cost		46,250
Gain		33,750

Task 9

(a)

Taxpayer	Sold to	Proceeds £	Market value £	Cost £	Other taxable income £	Capital Gains Tax £
Dave	Son	31,500	40,000	25,000	48,000	2,400
Brian	Wife	10,000	50,000	45,000	63,000	0
Sue	Friend	15,000	10,000	14,000	21,000	0
Alison	Friend	33,000	25,000	13,500	33,000	2,830

(b) £4,500

Working – the extended holiday counts as deemed occupation since it is preceded and followed by actual occupation. The last 9 months of ownership counts as deemed occupation.

Task 10

(a)

	Value of PET £
Gill gives Dave £5,000 to celebrate their forthcoming marriage	2,500
Roger donates £10,000 to the National Trust (a registered charity)	0
Sue gives her daughter £10,000 to help with a house deposit	10,000

(b) (a) False; (b) and (c) True

(c) £587,500

Working: £325,000 + £175,000 + (50% £175,000)

Answers to practice assessment 2

Task 1

(a) Tax avoidance is the legal use of claims and allowances to reduce the amount of tax payable. Tax evasion involves using illegal methods to reduce tax. There is a grey area between these two activities, and it is not always clear how HMRC or the courts will define a particular activity or scheme.

Where a scheme relies on concealment, pretence, non-disclosure or misrepresentation, this would be categorised as tax evasion which can result in criminal prosecution.

'Aggressive' tax avoidance schemes may also be examined under the General Anti-Abuse Rule (GAAR) legislation which will consider whether the law is being used in the way that Parliament originally anticipated.

If HMRC is aware of a particular scheme, it does not mean that HMRC has approved it as being legal. There could be ongoing investigations into the scheme which could result in it being declared illegal. Taxpayers must disclose their use of avoidance schemes, and will consequently be viewed as high risk individuals by HMRC. Their tax affairs may be subject to more scrutiny as a result.

Accountants should also consider their own ethical position when clients wish to undertake tax avoidance, and distance themselves from situations that do not meet their own or their professional body's ethical standards. They must also consider any reputational damage that may occur as a result of facilitating their clients' involvement in particular schemes.

(b) A progressive tax is one in which the proportion of the income of the individual or business that is charged as tax increases as the income increases.

Income Tax is a progressive tax, since the overall proportion of income that is tax increases the higher the income rises. This is due to the way that the combination of personal allowance, and basic rate, higher rate and additional rate taxes apply to an individual's total income.

A regressive tax is the opposite of a progressive tax. Here, the proportion of income that is charged as tax decreases as income increases.

Employees' NIC acts as a regressive tax for higher earners. This is because the rate changes from 8% to 2% at the upper earnings level of £50,270 per year, and this reduces the overall proportion of total income that is paid as employees' NIC for those earning above this amount.

Task 2

(a)

Car		%	£
Ford	Scale charge percentage	32	
	Taxable benefit on provision of the car		3,800
	Taxable benefit on provision of fuel		3,707
Citroen	Scale charge percentage	22	
	Taxable benefit on provision of the car		3,729
	Taxable benefit on provision of fuel		3,568
Total taxable benefit			14,804

(b)

	Engine type	CO_2 emissions	Scale charge %
Car 1	Petrol	143	33
Car 2	Electric	0	2

(c) (a) will result in an assessable benefit in kind; the other options will NOT.

(d)

	Assessable amount £
Use of computer games console	70
Interest-free loan	247
Mileage allowance	2,550

Task 3

(a) The tax payable on the dividends is **£498**

The tax payable on savings income is **£60**

The tax payable on dividend income is **£1,436**

(b)

Property	Taxable rent £	Allowable expenses £
12 Water Road	10,800	1,520
Upper Lodge	13,650	2,838
Manor House	12,600	2,420

(c)

Statement	True	False
The savings allowance can be set against dividend income where the individual has no savings income		✔
The cost of insuring a property during a period in between tenancies is an allowable property expense	✔	

Task 4

	Workings	£
Employment Income		97,500
Property Income	£6,060 - £8,100 = −£2,040 cf	0
Savings Income		780
Dividend Income		5,200
less personal allowance	£12,570 − ((£100,980 - £100,000) /2)	12,080
		91,400
General Income	£97,500 − £12,080 = £85,420	
	(£37,700 + (£2,000 / 0.8)) x 20%	8,040
	(£85,420 − £40,200) x 40%	18,088
Savings Income	£500 x 0% PSA	0
	£280 x 40%	112
Dividend Income	£500 x 0% DA	0
	£4,700 x 33.75%	1,586
Tax Liability		27,826

Task 5

(a)

	£
The total Class 1 NIC payable by Donna in the tax year	2,506
The total Class 1 NIC payable by Donna's employer in the tax year	4,802
The total Class 1A NIC payable by Donna's employer relating to the tax year	1,435

(b)

Statement	True	False
Employees' national insurance contributions are the same amounts for employees of all ages		✔
The employment allowance can be set against both employers' and employees' NIC		✔

Task 6

(a) (a) True; (b) False

(b) If the shares are bought in Paul's name, the tax payable on the dividends will be **£1,875** less than if they are bought in Cath's name.

If Joan spends an extra **£3,000** replacing a carpet in a rental property, she will save tax of £1,800.

If Roger changes this car to a petrol model with a CO_2 figure 35 g/km lower, it would save him annual tax on just the fuel benefit of **£1,223**.

Task 7

(a) (a), (b) and (d) True; (c) False

(b) (c) Loss of £1,000

(c)

	£
Proceeds or deemed proceeds	11,000
Cost or deemed cost	9,400
Gain or loss	1,600

Task 8

		Number of shares	Value £
April 2003	Purchase	800	3,000
May 2009	Purchase	1,200	4,680
December 2010	Rights issue	400	800
		2,400	8,480
November 2024	Disposal	500	1,767
	Balance	1,900	6,713
December 2024	Purchase	100	630
	Balance	2,000	7,343
		£	
	Proceeds	3,000	
	Cost	1,767	
	Gain	1,233	

Task 9

(a)

Taxpayer	Sold to	Proceeds £	Market value £	Cost £	Other taxable income £	Capital Gains Tax £
Adam	Cousin	41,500	50,000	29,000	58,000	1,900
Ben	Wife	35,000	40,000	20,000	23,000	0
Chloe	Stranger	25,000	28,000	12,000	21,000	1,000
Della	Friend	23,000	35,000	10,500	31,000	1,230

(b)

The amount chargeable to CGT in 2024/25 is	£9,700
The capital loss to be carried forward to 2025/26 is	£0

Task 10

(a)

	Value of PET £
Sue gives her daughter £12,000 to celebrate her marriage	1,000
Roger donates £20,000 to a qualifying political party	0
Richard gives his son £25,000 to help with a house deposit	19,000

(b) (b) True; (a) and (c) False

(c) The amount of the PET that is now chargeable to Inheritance Tax is **£75,000**

The amount of Inheritance Tax payable on the PET is **£6,000**

(working: 40% x 20% x £75,000)

The Inheritance Tax is payable **by the recipient of the PET**

Answers to practice assessment 3

Task 1

(a) Domicile is where an individual has their permanent home, and where they intend to stay for the future. Domicile can be changed by an individual moving to a different country, and demonstrating that they intend to live there permanently.

Residence is based on the country in which an individual is living during the tax year. There are precise rules that are used to determine residence separately for each tax year.

An individual who is UK resident, but not UK domiciled, will normally be subject to UK tax on their world-wide income and gains on an arising basis. They also have an option to be taxed on a remittance basis so that only income and gains brought into the UK are UK taxed. There is a substantial charge for this option.

(b) Caroline will meet the 'automatically resident' test. Although she is not in the UK for 183 days, she meets the alternative requirement as follows:

Caroline's only home was in the UK for over 91 days (in Caroline's case 148 days), and she lived there for over 30 days (again for 148 days).

Caroline is therefore a UK resident for 2024/25 without the need to apply any further tests.

Task 2

(a)

Car	Percentage applicable based on CO_2 emissions %	Cost of car used in benefit calculation £	Benefit in kind £
Jaguar	35	52,000	4,550
Range Rover	37	73,200	20,313
Total			24,863

(b)

	Engine type	CO_2 emissions	Scale charge %
Car 1	Diesel RDE2 compliant	142	33
Car 2	Petrol hybrid (electric range 45 miles)	25	8

(c) (c) will result in an assessable benefit in kind; the other options will NOT.

(d)

	Benefit £
On 6 April an employee was provided with an interest-free loan of £15,000. During the tax year he made three repayments, each of £2,000. The remainder of the loan was still outstanding at the end of the tax year.	270
On 6 April an employee was allowed the use of a home cinema system that had previously been used by the company. The home cinema had originally cost the company £1,500, but its market value on 6 April was £1,000.	200

Task 3

(a) The tax payable on the dividends is **£2,164**

The tax payable on savings income is **£330**

The tax payable on dividend income is **£1,923**

(b)

Property	Taxable rent £	Allowable expenses/ Property allowance £
1 Henry Road	11,400	1,000
Middle House	6,000	1,000
3 Lincoln Road	8,820	3,000

(c)

Statement	True	False
The adjusted net income can be used to help determine the level of personal savings allowance that is available in complex situations	✔	
The cost of renovating a property to bring it up to a suitable standard before it is first let out is not an allowable property expense	✔	

Task 4

	Workings	£
Employment Income		45,000
Property Income		8,150
Savings Income		1,780
Dividend Income		4,200
less Personal Allowance		12,570
		46,560
General Income £40,580	£45,000 + £8,150 − £12,570	
Basic rate tax	(£37,700 + £1,000) × 20%	7,740
Higher rate	(£40,580 − £38,700) × 40%	752
Savings Income £1,780	£500 × 0% PSA	0
	(£1,780 − £500) × 40%	512
Dividend Income £4,200	£500 × 0% DA	0
	£3,700 × 33.75%	1,248
Tax liability		10,252

Task 5

(a)

	£
The total Class 1 NIC payable by Ellen in the tax year	0
The total Class 1 NIC payable by Ellen's employer in the tax year	400
The total Class 1A NIC payable by Ellen's employer relating to the tax year	55

(b)

Statement	True	False
A cumulative income calculation is carried out to check that NIC for directors is not distorted by unusual payment patterns	✔	
Where total employers' NIC for an organisation is below £5,000, then HMRC will pay the difference between that figure and £5,000 to the organisation		✔

answers to practice assessment 3

Task 6

(a) Both statements are True

(b) If the monthly interest option is chosen, then over the two tax years Peter will pay **£160** less tax on savings income than if the annual interest option is chosen.

If Jo earned a further £1,000 as an employment bonus, her tax would increase by **£600**.

In a full tax year, this would save Roland Income Tax of **£416**.

Task 7

(a)

	Amount £
Proceeds	15,000
Total costs	14,940
Gain	60

(b) (a), (c) and (d) True; (b) and (e) False

(c) The amount subject to Capital Gains Tax for the year (after the annual exempt amount) will be **£2,400**.

The capital loss to be carried forward to be set against future gains will be **£0**.

Task 8

October 2000	18,000	£81,000
April 2012	8,000	£24,000
	26,000	£105,000
Disposal	12,000	£48,462
Pool balance	14,000	£56,538
Proceeds		£72,000
Cost		£48,462
Gain		£23,538

Task 9

(a)

Taxpayer	Sold to	Proceeds £	Market value £	Cost £	Other taxable income £	Capital Gains Tax £
Ella	Grandfather	48,500	55,000	24,000	58,000	5,600
Fred	Civil Partner	29,000	40,000	12,000	20,000	0
Gareth	Stranger	25,000	20,000	10,000	22,000	1,200
Helen	Friend	20,000	32,000	8,500	45,000	1,700

(b)

The amount chargeable to CGT in 2024/25 is	£11,550
The capital loss to be carried forward to 2025/26 is	£0

Task 10

(a)

	Value of PET £
Stan gives his son £15,000 to celebrate his marriage	4,000
Ron donates £2,000 to a museum	0
Robert gives his nephew £15,000 to help with a house deposit	9,000

(b) (a) and (c) True; (b) False

(c) The nil rate band available at death will be **£175,000**

The rate of Inheritance Tax charged on the relevant part of the death estate will be **36%**

The Inheritance Tax payable due to Michelle's death must be paid by the following date **31 August 2025**

Reference Material

for AAT Assessment of Personal Tax

Finance Act 2024

For assessments from 27 January 2025

Note: this reference material is accessible by candidates during their live computer based assessment for Personal Tax.

This material was current at the time this book was published, but may be subject to change. Readers are advised to check the AAT website or Osborne Books website for any updates.

Introduction

This document comprises data that you may need to consult during your Personal Tax computer-based assessment.

The material can be consulted during the practice and live assessments by using the reference materials section at each task position. It's made available here so you can familiarise yourself with the content before the assessment.

Do not take a print of this document into the exam room with you*.

This document may be changed to reflect periodical updates in the computer-based assessment, so please check you have the most recent version while studying.

This version is based on **Finance Act 2024** and is for use in AAT Q2022 assessments from **27 January 2025.**

*Unless you need a printed version as part of reasonable adjustments for particular needs, in which case you must discuss this with your tutor at least six weeks before the assessment date.

> Note that page numbers refer to those in the original AAT Guidance document

Contents

1.	**Tax Rate and bands**	4
2.	**Allowances**	4
3.	**Property income allowance**	4
4.	**Individual savings accounts**	4
5.	**Deemed domicile**	5
6.	**Residence**	5
7.	**Car benefit percentage**	6
8.	**Car fuel benefit**	6
9.	**Approved mileage allowance payments (employees and residential landlords)**	6
10.	**Van benefit charge**	7
11.	**Other benefits kind**	7
12.	**HMRC official rate**	8
13.	**National insurance contributions**	8
14.	**Capital gains tax**	8
15.	**Capital gains tax – tax rates**	8
16.	**Inheritance tax – tax rates**	9
17.	**Inheritance tax – tapering relief**	9
18.	**Inheritance tax – exemptions**	9

1. Tax Rate and bands

Tax rates	Tax bands	Normal rates %	Dividend rates %
Basic rate	£1 – £37,700	20	8.75
Higher rate	£37,701 – £125,140	40	33.75
Additional rate	£125,141 and over	45	39.35

2. Allowances

		£
Personal allowance		12,570
Savings allowance:	Basic rate taxpayer	1,000
	Higher rate taxpayer	500
Dividend allowance		500
Income limit for personal allowances*		100,000

* Personal allowances are reduced by £1 for every £2 over the income limit.

3. Property income allowance

	£
Annual limit	1,000

4. Individual savings accounts

	£
Annual limit	20,000

5. Deemed domicile

Deemed domicile	Criteria
Condition A	Was born in the UK
	Domicile of origin was in the UK
	Was resident in the UK for the tax year in question
Condition B	Has been UK resident for at least 15 of the 20 tax years immediately before the relevant tax year

6. Residence

Residence	Criteria
Automatically not resident	Spend fewer than 16 days in the UK (or 46 days if you have not been classed as UK resident for the three previous tax years; or
	Work abroad full time (averaging at least 35 hours a week) and spend less than 91 days in the UK, of which no more than 30 are spent working
Automatically resident	Spend 183 or more days in the UK in the tax year; or
	Only home is in the UK; and
	You owned, rented or lived in the home for at least 91 days and spent at least 30 days there in the tax year.
Resident by number of ties	If UK resident for one or more of the previous three tax years: • 4 ties needed if spend 16-45 days in the UK • 3 ties needed if spend 46-90 days in the UK • 2 ties needed if spend 91-120 days in the UK • 1 tie needed if spend over 120 days in the UK. If UK resident in none of the previous three tax years: • 4 ties needed if spend 46-90 days in the UK • 3 ties needed if spend 91-120 days in the UK • 2 ties needed if spend over 120 days in the UK.

7. Car benefit percentage

CO_2 Emissions for petrol engines g/km	Electric range (miles)	%
Nil	NA	2
1 to 50	130 or more	2
1 to 50	70-129	5
1 to 50	40-69	8
1 to 50	30-39	12
1 to 50	Less than 30	14
51 to 54		15
55 or more		16 + 1% for every extra 5g/km above 55g/km
Diesel engines*		Additional 4%

*The additional 4% will not apply to diesel cars which are registered after 1 September 2017 and meet the RDE2 standards.

8. Car fuel benefit

	£
Base figure	27,800

9. Approved mileage allowance payments (employees and residential landlords)

First 10,000 miles	45p per mile
Over 10,000 miles	25p per mile
Additional passengers	5p per mile per passenger
Motorcycles	24p per mile
Bicycles	20p per mile

10. Van benefit charge

	£
Basic charge	3,960
Private fuel charge	757
Benefit charge for zero emission vans	NIL

11. Other benefits in kind

Benefit	Notes
Expensive accommodation limit	£75,000
Health screening	One per year
Incidental overnight expenses: within UK	£5 per night
Incidental overnight expenses: overseas	£10 per night
Job-related accommodation	£Nil
Living expenses where job-related exemption applies	Restricted to 10% of employees net earnings
Loan of assets annual charge	20%
Low-rate or interest free loans	Up to £10,000
Mobile telephones	One per employee
Non-cash gifts from someone other than the employer	£250 per tax year
Non-cash long service award	£50 per year of service
Pay whilst attending a full-time course	£15,480 per academic year
Provision of eye tests and spectacles for DSE (display screen equipment)	£Nil
Provision of parking spaces	£Nil
Provision of workplace childcare	£Nil
Provision of workplace sports facilities	£Nil
Removal and relocation expenses	£8,000
Staff party or event	£150 per head
Staff suggestion scheme	Up to £5,000
Subsidised meals	£Nil
Working from home	£6 per week/£26 per month

12. HMRC official rate

	%
HMRC official rate	2.25

13. National insurance contributions

		%
Class 1 Employee:	Below £12,570	0
	Above £12,570 and below £50,270	8
	£50,270 and above	2
Class 1 Employer:	Below £9,100	0
	£9,100 and above	13.8
Class 1A		13.8

	£
Employment allowance	5,000

14. Capital gains tax

	£
Annual exempt amount	3,000

15. Capital gains tax – tax rates

	%
Basic rate	10
Higher rate	20

16. Inheritance tax – tax rates

		£
Nil rate band		325,000
Additional residence nil-rate band*		175,000
		%
Excess taxable at:	Death rate	40
	Lifetime rate	20

*Applies when a home is passed on death to direct descendants of the deceased after 6 April 2017. Any unused band is transferrable to a spouse or civil partner.

17. Inheritance tax – tapering relief

	% reduction
3 years or less	0
Over 3 years but less than 4 years	20
Over 4 years but less than 5 years	40
Over 5 years but less than 6 years	60
Over 6 years but less than 7 years	80

18. Inheritance tax – exemptions

		£
Small gifts		250 per transferee per tax year
Marriage or civil partnership:	From parent	5,000
	Grandparent	2,500
	One party to the other	2,500
	Others	1,000
Annual exemption		3,000

Reference Material

for AAT Assessment of Personal Tax

Finance Act 2024

Professional conduct in relation to taxation

For assessments from 27 January 2025

Note: this reference material is accessible by candidates during their live computer based assessment for Personal Tax.

This material was current at the time this book was published, but may be subject to change. Readers are advised to check the AAT website or Osborne Books website for any updates.

Reference material for AAT assessment of Personal Tax

Introduction

This document comprises data that you may need to consult during your Personal Tax computer-based assessment.

The material can be consulted during the practice and live assessments by using the reference material section at each task position. It is made available here so you can familiarise yourself with the content before the assessment.

Do not take a print of this document into the exam room with you*.

This document may be changed to reflect periodical updates in the computer-based assessment, so please check you have the most recent version while studying.

This version is based on **Finance Act 2024** and is for use in AAT assessments from **27 January 2025**.

* Unless you need a printed version as part of reasonable adjustments for particular needs, in which case you must discuss this with your tutor at least six weeks before the assessment date.

> Note that page numbers refer to those in the original AAT Guidance document

Contents

1.	Interpretation and abbreviations	4
2.	Fundamental principles	5
3.	PCRT Help sheet A: Submission of tax information and 'Tax filings'	6
4.	PCRT Help sheet B: Tax advice	10
5.	PCRT Help sheet C: Dealing with errors	12
6.	PCRT Help sheet D: Requests for data by HMRC	15

1. Interpretation and abbreviations

Context

Tax advisors operate in a complex business and financial environment. The increasing public focus on the role of taxation in wider society means a greater interest in the actions of tax advisors and their clients.

This guidance, written by the professional bodies for their members working in tax, sets out the hallmarks of a good tax advisor, and in particular the fundamental principles of behaviour that members are expected to follow.

Interpretation

1.1 In this guidance:
- 'Client' includes, where the context requires, 'former client'
- 'Member' (and 'members') includes 'firm' or 'practice' and the staff thereof
- 'Word' in the singular include the plural and 'words' in the plural include the singular.

Abbreviations

1.1 The following abbreviations have been used:

AML	Anti-Money Laundering
CCAB	Consultative Committee of Accountancy Bodies
DOTAS	Disclosure of Tax Avoidance Schemes
GAAP	Generally Accepted Accounting Principles
GAAR	General Anti-Abuse Rule in Finance Act 2013
GDPR	General Data Protection Regulation
HMRC	Her Majesty's Revenue and Customs
MTD	Making Tax Digital
MLRO	Money Laundering Reporting Officer
NCA	National Crime Agency (previously the Serious Organised Crime Agency
POTAS	Promoters of Tax Avoidance Schemes
PCRT	Professional Conduct in Relation to Taxation
SRN	Scheme Reference Number

2. Fundamental principles

Overview of the fundamental principles

1. Ethical behaviour in the tax profession is critical. The work carried out by a member needs to be trusted by society at large as well as by clients and other stakeholders. What a member does reflects not just on themselves but on the profession as a whole.

2. A member must comply with the following fundamental principles:

   Integrity

   To be straightforward and honest in all professional and business relationships.

   Objectivity

   To not allow bias, conflict of interest or undue influence of others to override professional or business judgements.

   Professional competence and due care

   To maintain professional knowledge and skill at the level required to ensure that a client or employer receives competent professional service based on current developments in practice, legislation and techniques and act diligently and in accordance with applicable technical and professional standards.

   Confidentiality

   To respect the confidentiality of information acquired as a result of professional and business relationships and, therefore, not disclose any such information to third parties without proper and specific authority, unless there is a legal or professional right or duty to disclose, nor use the information for the personal advantage of the member or third parties.

   Professional behaviour

   To comply with relevant laws and regulations and avoid any action that discredits the profession.

3. PCRT Help sheet A: Submission of tax information and 'Tax filings'

Definition of filing of tax information and tax filings (filing)

1. For the purposes of this guidance, the term 'filing' includes any online submission of data, online filing or other filing that is prepared on behalf of the client for the purposes of disclosing to any taxing authority details that are to be used in the calculation of tax due by a client or a refund of tax due to the client or for other official purposes. It includes all taxes, NIC and duties.

2. A letter, or online notification, giving details in respect of a filing or as an amendment to a filing including, for example, any voluntary disclosure of an error should be dealt with as if it was a filing.

Making Tax Digital and filing

3. Tax administration systems, including the UK's, are increasingly moving to mandatory digital filing of tax information and returns.

4. Except in exceptional circumstances, a member will explicitly file in their capacity as agent. A member is advised to use the facilities provided for agents and to avoid knowing or using the client's personal access credentials.

5. A member should keep their access credentials safe from unauthorised use and consider periodic change of passwords.

6. A member is recommended to forward suspicious emails to phishing@hmrc.gsi.gov.uk and then delete them. It is also important to avoid clicking on websites or links in suspicious emails, or opening attachments.

7. Firms should have policies on cyber security, AML and GDPR.

Taxpayer's responsibility

8. The taxpayer has primary responsibility to submit correct and complete filings to the best of their knowledge and belief. The final decision as to whether to disclose any issue is that of the client but in relation to your responsibilities see paragraph 12 below.

9. In annual self-assessment returns or returns with short filing periods the filing may include reasonable estimates where necessary.

Member's responsibility

10. A member who prepares a filing on behalf of a client is responsible to the client for the accuracy of the filing based on the information provided.

11. In dealing with HMRC in relation to a client's tax affairs a member should bear in mind their duty of confidentiality to the client and that they are acting as the agent of their client. They have a duty to act in the best interests of their client.

12. A member should act in good faith in dealings with HMRC in accordance with the fundamental principle of integrity. In particular the member should take reasonable care and exercise appropriate professional scepticism when making statements or asserting facts on behalf of a client.

13. Where acting as a tax agent, a member is not required to audit the figures in the books and records provided or verify information provided by a client or by a third party. However, a member should take care not to be associated with the presentation of facts they know or believe to be incorrect or misleading, not to assert tax positions in a tax filing which they consider to have no sustainable basis.

14. When a member is communicating with HMRC, they should consider whether they need to make it clear to what extent they are relying on information which has been supplied by the client or a third party.

Materiality

15. Whether an amount is to be regarded as material depends upon the facts and circumstances of each case.

16. The profits of a trade, profession, vocation or property business should be computed in accordance with GAAP subject to any adjustment required or authorised by law in computing profits for those purposes. This permits a trade, profession, vocation or property business to disregard non-material adjustments in computing its accounting profits.

17. The application of GAAP, and therefore materiality, does not extend beyond the accounting profits. Thus, the accounting concept of materiality cannot be applied when completing tax filings.

18. It should be noted that for certain small businesses an election may be made to use the cash basis instead; for small property businesses the default position is the cash basis. Where the cash basis is used, materiality is not relevant.

Disclosure

19. If a client is unwilling to include in a tax filing the minimum information required by law, the member should follow the guidance in Help sheet C: Dealing with Errors. The paragraphs below (paras 20 – 24) give guidance on some of the more common areas of uncertainty over disclosure.

20. In general, it is likely to be in a client's own interests to ensure that factors relevant to their tax liability are adequately disclosed to HMRC because:
    - their relationship with HMRC is more likely to be on a satisfactory footing if they can demonstrate good faith in their dealings with them. HMRC notes in 'Your Charter' that 'We want to give you a service that is fair, accurate and based on mutual trust and respect'
    - they will reduce the risk of a discovery or further assessment and may reduce exposure to interest and penalties.

21. It may be advisable to consider fuller disclosure than is strictly necessary. Reference to 'The Standards for Tax Planning' in PCRT may be relevant. The factors involved in making this decision include:
    - a filing relies on a valuation
    - the terms of the applicable law
    - the view taken by the member
    - the extent of any doubt that exists
    - the manner in which disclosure is to be made
    - the size and gravity of the item in question.

22. When advocating fuller disclosure than is necessary a member should ensure that their client is adequately aware of the issues involved and their potential implications. Fuller disclosure should only be made with the client's consent.

23. Cases will arise where there is doubt as to the correct treatment of an item of income or expenditure, or the computation of a gain or allowance. In such cases a member ought to consider what additional disclosure, if any, might be necessary. For example, additional disclosure should be considered where:
    - there is inherent doubt as to the correct treatment of an item, for example, expenditure on repairs which might be regarded as capital in whole or part, or the VAT liability of a particular transaction, or
    - HMRC has published its interpretation or has indicated its practice on a point, but the client proposes to adopt a different view, whether or not supported by Counsel's opinion. The member should refer to the guidance on the Veltema case and the paragraph below. See also HMRC guidance.

24. A member who is uncertain whether their client should disclose a particular item or of its treatment should consider taking further advice before reaching a decision. They should use their best endeavours to ensure that the client understands the issues, implications and the proposed course of action. Such a decision may have to be justified at a later date, so the member's files should contain sufficient evidence to support the position taken, including timely notes of discussions with the client and/or with other advisors, copies of any second opinion obtained and the client's final decision. A failure to take reasonable care may result in HMRC imposing a penalty if an error is identified after an enquiry.

Supporting documents

25. For the most part, HMRC does not consider that it is necessary for a taxpayer to provide supporting documentation in order to satisfy the taxpayer's overriding need to make a correct filing. HMRC's view is that, where it is necessary for that purpose, explanatory information should be entered in the 'white space' provided on the filing. However, HMRC does recognise that the taxpayer may wish to supply further details of a particular computation or transaction in order to minimise the risk of a discovery assessment being raised at a later time. Following the uncertainty created by the decision in Veltema, HMRC's guidance can be found in SP1/06 – Self Assessment: Finality and Discovery.

26. Further HMRC guidance says that sending attachments with a tax filing is intended for those cases where the taxpayer 'feels it is crucial to provide additional information to support the filing but for some reason cannot utilise the white space'.

Reliance on HMRC published guidance

27. Whilst it is reasonable in most circumstances to rely on HMRC published guidance, a member should be aware that the Tribunal and the courts will apply the law even if this conflicts with HMRC guidance.

28. Notwithstanding this, if a client has relied on HMRC guidance which is clear and unequivocal and HMRC resiles from any of the terms of the guidance, a Judicial Review claim is a possible route to pursue.

Approval of tax filings

29. The member should advise the client to review their tax filing before it is submitted.

30. The member should draw the client's attention to the responsibility which the client is taking in approving the filing as correct and complete. Attention should be drawn to any judgmental areas or positions reflected in the filing to ensure that the client is aware of these and their implications before they approve the filing.

31. A member should obtain evidence of the client's approval of the filing in electronic or non-electronic form.

4. PCRT Help sheet B: Tax advice

The Standards for Tax Planning

1. The Standards for Tax Planning are critical to any planning undertaken by members. They are:

    - Client Specific

        Tax planning must be specific to the particular client's facts and circumstances. Clients must be alerted to the wider risks and implications of any courses of action.

    - Lawful

        At all times members must act lawfully and with integrity and expect the same from their clients. Tax planning should be based on a realistic assessment of the facts and on a credible view of the law.

        Members should draw their client's attention to where the law is materially uncertain, for example because HMRC is known to take a different view of the law. Members should consider taking further advice appropriate to the risks and circumstances of the particular case, for example where litigation is likely.

    - Disclosure and transparency

        Tax advice must not rely for its effectiveness on HMRC having less than the relevant facts. Any disclosure must fairly represent all relevant facts.

    - Tax planning arrangements

        Members must not create, encourage or promote tax planning arrangements or structures that i) set out to achieve results that are contrary to the clear intention of Parliament in enacting relevant legislation and/or ii) are highly artificial or highly contrived and seek to exploit shortcomings within the relevant legislation.

    - Professional judgement and appropriate documentation

        Applying these requirements to particular client advisory situations requires members to exercise professional judgement on a number of matters. Members should keep notes on a timely basis of the rationale for the judgements exercised in seeking to adhere to these requirements

Guidance

2. The paragraphs below provide guidance for members when considering whether advice complies with the Fundamental Principles and Standards for Tax Planning.

Tax evasion

3. A member should never be knowingly involved in tax evasion, although, of course, it is appropriate to act for a client who is rectifying their affairs.

Tax planning and advice

4. In contrast to tax evasion, tax planning is legal. However, under the Standard members 'must not create, encourage or promote tax planning arrangements that (i) set out to achieve results that are contrary to the clear intention of Parliament in enacting relevant legislation and/or (ii) are highly artificial or highly contrived and seek to exploit shortcomings within the relevant legislation'.

5. Things to consider:
    - have you checked that your engagement letter fully covers the scope of the planning advice?
    - have you taken the Standards for Tax Planning and the Fundamental Principles into account? Is it client specific? Is it lawful? Will all relevant facts be disclosed to HMRC? Is it creating, encouraging, or promoting tax planning contrary to the 4th Standard for Tax Planning?
    - how tax sophisticated is the client?
    - has the client made clear what they wish to achieve by the planning?
    - what are the issues involved with the implementation of the planning?
    - what are the risks associated with the planning and have you warned the client of them? For example:
        - the strength of the legal interpretation relied upon
        - the potential application of the GAAR
        - the implications for the client, including the obligations of the client in relation to their tax return, if the planning requires disclosure under DOTAS or DASVOIT and the potential for an accelerated payment notice or partner payment notice?
        - the reputational risk to the client and the member of the planning in the public arena
        - the stress, cost and wider personal or business implications to the client in the event of a prolonged dispute with HMRC. This may involve unwelcomed publicity, costs, expenses and loss of management time over a significant period

- if the client tenders for government contracts, the potential impact of the proposed tax planning on tendering for and retaining public sector contracts
- the risk of counteraction. This may occur before the planning is completed or potentially there may be retrospective counteraction at a later date
- the risk of challenge by HMRC. Such challenge may relate to the legal interpretation relied upon, but may alternatively relate to the construction of the facts, including the implementation of the planning
- the risk and inherent uncertainty of litigation. The probability of the planning being overturned by the courts if litigated and the potential ultimate downside should the client be unsuccessful
- is a second opinion necessary/advisable?

- are the arrangements in line with any applicable code of conduct or ethical guidelines or stances, for example the Banking Code, and fit and proper tests for charity trustees and pension administrators?
- are you satisfied that the client understands the planning proposed?
- have you documented the advice given and the reasoning behind it?

5. PCRT Help sheet C: Dealing with errors

Introduction

1. For the purposes of this guidance, the term 'error' is intended to include all errors and mistakes whether they were made by the client, the member, HMRC or any other party involved in a client's tax affairs, and whether made innocently or deliberately.

2. During a member's relationship with the client, the member may become aware of possible errors in the client's tax affairs. Unless the client is already aware of the possible error, they should be informed as soon as the member identifies them.

3. Where the error has resulted in the client paying too much tax the member should advise the client to make a repayment claim. The member should advise the client of the time limits to make a claim and have regard to any relevant time limits. The rest of this Help sheet deals with situations where tax may be due to HMRC.

4. Sometimes an error made by HMRC may mean that the client has not paid tax actually due or they have been incorrectly repaid tax. There may be fee costs as a result of correcting such mistakes. A member should bear in mind that, in some circumstances, clients or agents may be able to claim for additional professional costs incurred and compensation from HMRC.

5. A member should act correctly from the outset. A member should keep sufficient appropriate records of discussions and advice and when dealing with errors the member should:
   - give the client appropriate advice
   - if necessary, so long as they continue to act for the client, seek to persuade the client to behave correctly
   - take care not to appear to be assisting a client to plan or commit any criminal offence or to conceal any offence which has been committed
   - in appropriate situations, or where in doubt, discuss the client's situation with a colleague or an independent third party (having due regard to client confidentiality).

6. Once aware of a possible error, a member must bear in mind the legislation on money laundering and the obligations and duties which this places upon them.

7. Where the member may have made the error, the member should consider whether they need to notify their professional indemnity insurers.

8. In any situation where a member has concerns about their own position, they should consider taking specialist legal advice. For example, where a client appears to have used the member to assist in the commissioning of a criminal offence and people could question whether the member had acted honestly in good faith. Note that The Criminal Finances Act 2017 has created new criminal offences of failure to prevent facilitation of tax evasion.

9. The flowchart below summarises the recommended steps a member should take where a possible error arises. It must be read in conjunction with the guidance and commentary that follow it.

Dealing with errors flowchart

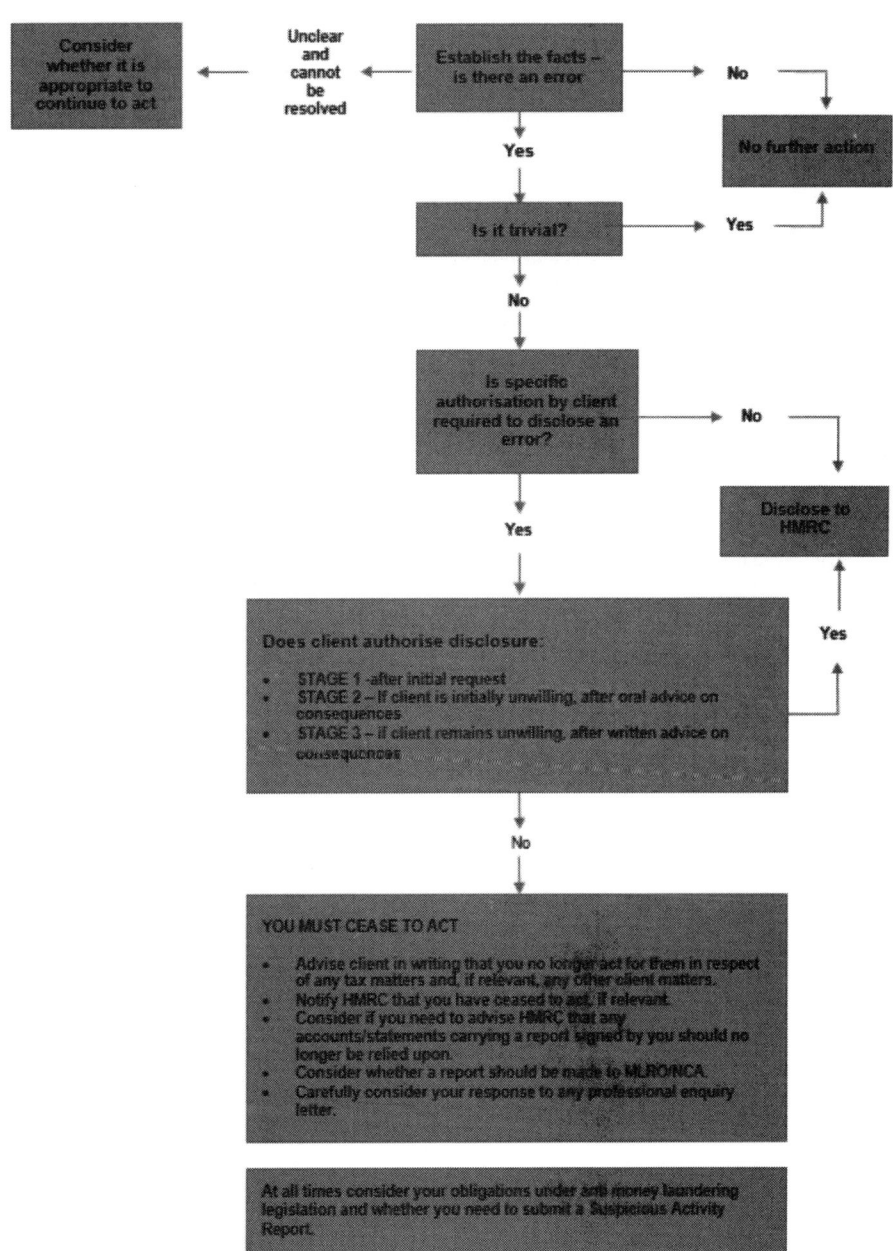

6. PCRT Help sheet D: Requests for data by HMRC

Introduction

1. For the purposes of this help sheet the term 'data' includes documents in whatever form (including electronic) and other information. While this guidance relates to HMRC requests, other government bodies or organisations may also approach the member for data. The same principles apply.

2. A distinction should be drawn between a request for data made informally ('informal requests') and those requests for data which are made in exercise of a power to require the provision of the data requested ('formal requests').

3. Similarly, requests addressed to a client and those addressed to a member require different handling.

4. Where a member no longer acts for a client, the member remains subject to the duty of confidentiality. In relation to informal requests, the member should refer the enquirer either to the former client or if authorised by the client to the new agent. In relation to formal requests addressed to the member, the termination of their professional relationship with the client does not affect the member's duty to comply with that request, where legally required to do so.

5. A member should comply with formal requests and should not seek to frustrate legitimate requests for information. Adopting a constructive approach may help to resolve issues promptly and minimise costs to all parties.

6. Whilst a member should be aware of HMRC's powers it may be appropriate to take specialist advice.

7. Devolved tax authorities have separate powers.

8. Two flowcharts are at the end of this help sheet:
    - requests for data addressed to the member
    - requests for data addressed to the client.

Informal requests addressed to the client

9. From time to time, HMRC chooses to communicate directly with clients rather than with the appointed agent.

10. HMRC has given reassurances that it is working to ensure that initial contact on compliance checks will normally be via the agent and only if the agent does not reply within an appropriate timescale will the contact be directly with the client.

11. When the member assists a client in dealing with such requests from HMRC, the member should advise the client that cooperation with informal requests can provide greater opportunities for the taxpayer to find a pragmatic way to work through the issue at hand with HMRC.

Informal requests addressed to the member

12. Disclosure in response to informal requests can only be made with the client's permission.

13. In many instances, the client will have authorised routine disclosure of relevant data, for example, through the engagement letter. However, if there is any doubt about whether the client has authorised disclosure, the member should ask the client to approve what is to be disclosed.

14. Where an oral enquiry is made by HMRC, a member should consider asking for it to be put in writing so that a response may be agreed with the client.

15. Although there is no obligation to comply with an informal request in whole or in part, a member should advise the client whether it is in the client's best interests to disclose such data, as lack of cooperation may have a direct impact on penalty negotiations post—enquiry.

16. Informal requests may be forerunners to formal requests compelling the disclosure of data. Consequently, it may be sensible to comply with such requests.

Formal requests addressed to the client

17. In advising their client a member should consider whether specialist advice may be needed, for example on such issues as whether the notice has been issued in accordance with the relevant tax legislation and whether the data request is valid.

18. The member should also advise the client about any relevant right of appeal against the formal request if appropriate and of the consequences of a failure to comply.

19. If the notice is legally effective the client is legally obliged to comply with the request.

20. The most common statutory notice issued to clients and third parties by HMRC is under Schedule 36 FA 2008.

Formal requests addressed to the member

21. The same principles apply to formal requests to the member as formal requests to clients.

22. If a formal request is valid it **overrides the member's duty of confidentiality** to their client. The member is therefore obliged to comply with the request. Failure to comply with their legal obligations can expose the member to civil or criminal penalties.

23. In cases where the member is not legally precluded by the terms of the notice from communicating with the client, the member should advise the client of the notice and keep the client informed of progress and developments.

24. The member should ensure that in complying with any notice they do not provide information or data outside the scope of the notice.

25. If a member is faced with a situation in which HMRC is seeking to enforce disclosure by the removal of data, or seeking entrance to inspect business premises occupied by a member in their capacity as an adviser, the member should consider seeking immediate professional advice, to ensure that this is the legally correct course of action.

Privileged data

26. Legal privilege arises under common law and may only be overridden if this is set out in legislation. It protects a party's right to communicate in confidence with a legal adviser. The privilege belongs to the client and not to the member.

27. If a document is privileged: The client cannot be required to make disclosure of that document to HMRC. Another party cannot disclose it (including the member), without the client's express permission.

28. There are two types of legal privilege under common law: legal advice privilege and litigation privilege.

(a) **Legal advice privilege**

Covers documents passing between a client and their legal adviser prepared for the purposes of obtaining or giving legal advice. However, communications from a tax adviser who is not a practising lawyer will not attract legal advice privilege even if such individuals are giving advice on legal matters such as tax law.

(b) **Litigation privilege**

Covers data created for the dominant purpose of litigation. Litigation privilege may arise where litigation has not begun but is merely contemplated and may apply to data prepared by non-lawyer advisors (including tax advisors). There are two important limits on litigation privilege. First, it does not arise in respect of non-adversarial proceedings. Second, the documents must be produced for the 'dominant purpose' of litigation.

29. A privilege under Schedule 36 paragraphs 19, (documents relating to the conduct of a pending appeal), 24 and 25 (auditors, and tax advisors' documents) might exist by "quasi-privilege" and if this is the case a tax adviser does not have to provide those documents. Care should be taken as not all data may be privileged.

30. A member who receives a request for data, some of which the member believes may be subject to privilege or 'quasi-privilege', should take independent legal advice on the position, unless expert in this area.

Help sheet D: Flowchart regarding requests for data by HMRC to the Member

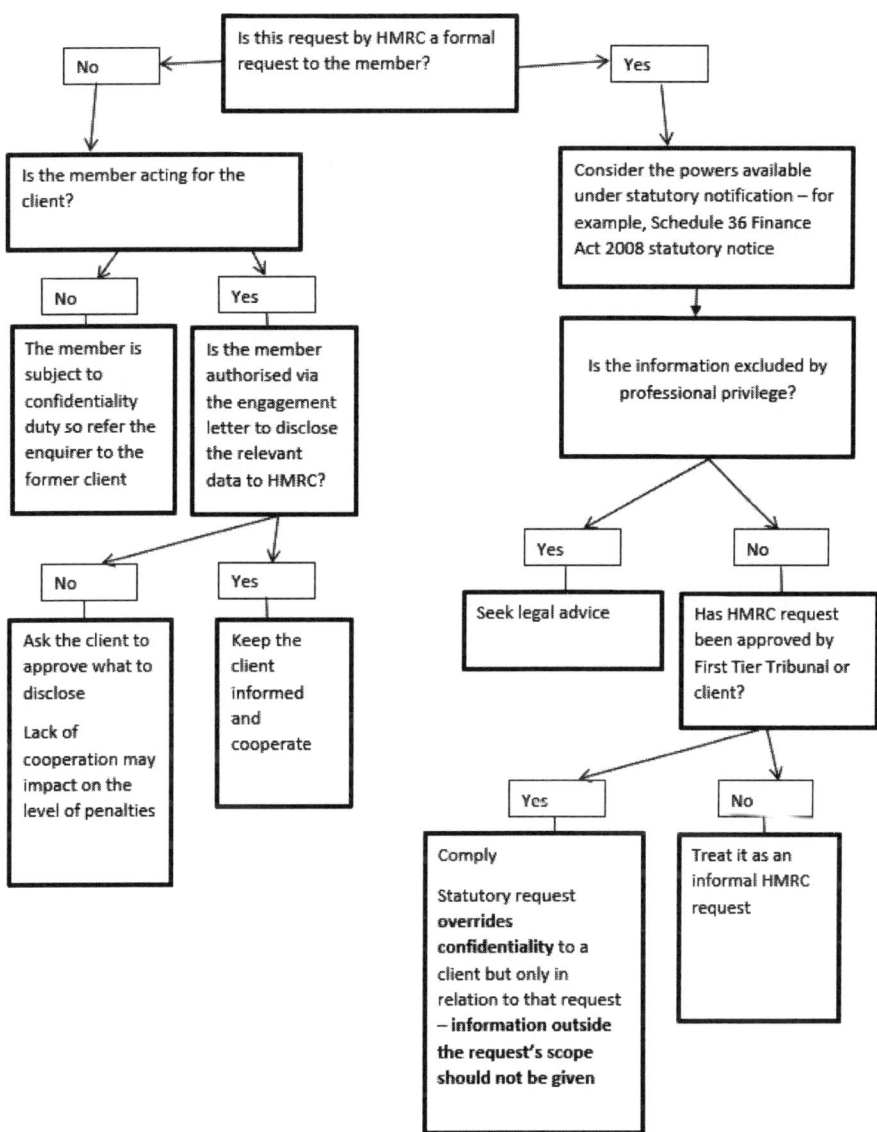

Flowchart regarding requests for data by HMRC to the Client

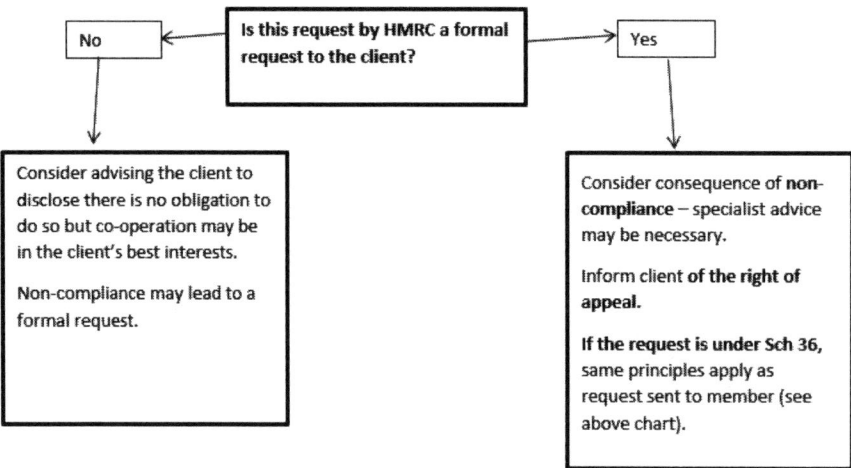

AAT
30 Churchill Place
London E14 5RE

aat.org.uk

AAT is a registered charity. No. 1050724

for your notes

for your notes

for your notes

for your notes

for your notes

for your notes

for your notes

for your notes

for your notes

for your notes

for your notes

for your notes

for your notes